# THE MIRACLE MAN

## THE LIFE STORY OF JOAO DE DEUS

### By Robert Pellegrino-Estrich

TRIAD

For information address:
TRIAD Publishers Pty.Ltd.
P.O. Box 731
Cairns, Qld. 4870
Australia
Ph: (07) 4093 0121
Fax: (07) 4093 0374
E-mail address: triad@austarnet.com.au
Web site: http://www.triadpublishers.com

**Book Title:**
THE MIRACLE MAN
**Author:**
Robert Pellegrino-Estrich

**National Library Of Australia: ISBN: 0 646 33767 X**
Printed in Australia

*Triad publications aim at aiding and inspiring
a spiritually unfolding humanity*

"For Those Who Believe,
No Words Are Necessary:
For Those Who Do Not Believe,
No Words Are Possible."

*Dom Inacio de Loyola.*

To Joao Teixeira da Faria and his Entities who cured my heart and awakened my soul, and in so doing, showed me the way 'home'. The writing of this book and the delivery of your message to all humanity was not a task, it was a privilege.

My only hope is that my ability to write does justice to your abiltity to heal. I am eternally grateful for the opportunity to guide so many people to this God-gifted healer – as much for the enhancement of their soul as for the treatment of their body.

*Robert Pellegrino-Estrich*

# Contents

# Acknowledgements

My thanks to two people, without whom this book might not have eventuated:

Caterina, my wife, whose gifted knowledge of spiritual reality, gained from previous lives, was invaluable as a guide of all things spiritual and its relationship to physical life; and my son Scott whose knowledge of computers greatly exceeds mine and his natural understanding of life's facets which, together with Caterina, enabled me to see the bigger picture – the help this book would provide to those in need of physical, emotional or spiritual guidance.

## Author's Note

Whilst there are many "instantaneous" and seemingly "miraculous" healings at the Casa de Dom Inacio, it should be noted that most healings take time - there is no way of knowing how long before results are clearly observable. Some are obvious within weeks, some in a few months and some require much longer with more than one visit.

Most people, depending on the stage and gravity of their illness, respond favourably - some, however, do not. A missing limb cannot be replaced and similarly, a severely degenerated organism might not respond - there is a point beyond which the body cannot regenerate. The ability to respond favourably is dependent upon many things including the effects of medication, physical deterioration of the body, spiritual awareness and in some cases karma.

WARNING:

If you are gravely ill do not risk the long journey, it is not wise to risk hospitalisation in Brazil. If you die it places an unbearable strain on your carers, on Joao and the "house ".

I have been richly rewarded by the feedback from those people who have received a second chance at life at the Casa de Dom Inacio. My only request to those who seek solace there is to show the "house" and the people who compassionately give their time in its function the respect they deserve: dress modestly in white pants, not shorts. Be patient and respectful - it's a house of God run mainly by humanitarian volunteers. Don't be demanding – it is not a public hospital. Have respect for this remarkable man who gives his time and his body to offer you a second chance. His entities can do just so much; you must do your part too!

# Foreword

Thoughts of our origins and the purpose of our existence most often occur in that brief moment before we slide into sleep state. When our day's work is done, we've watched the six o'clock news and grown weary from too much television. In that dark waiting state, between "lights out" and the welcome veil of sleep, our minds will often query the reason for our being. I know I did!

I was just like you; hard working, dedicated, ambitious and, after twenty five years of twelve hour days, I felt I had made it; a successful businessman, the proud owner of several jewellery stores. I enjoyed the fruits of my labour; a large waterfront home, luxury apartment on the beach, investment properties, a Mercedes Benz and private schooling for my two sons. But deep inside me I often felt that life must have a greater purpose. Surely this could not be all there was to it. Then one day, quite unexpectedly, the "Lord tooketh away". Actually it wasn't the Lord but some "low life", a common thief who robbed one of my stores and reduced my materially wonderful life to rubble.

As I sat staring at my empty sstore contemplating the consequences of an insurance policy that would not cover the circumstance, I had the first glimpse of how fragile, how futile a purely material life really is.

t was in the following bleak months of receivership that I was forced to look for a deeper meaning to life. When the world finally stopped spinning and all I held dear was gone; marriage, wealth, properties, income and, most of all, my self worth It was time to look for another meaning. Not, I hasten to add, the ritualism of modern religions or the zealous fanaticism of the "new born" breed. My years of calculated commercialism left me with a permanent factual attitude to life so I needed evidence in cold hard facts to support any new beliefs. I have been given the opportunity to observe at first hand irrefutable proof of the reason for our existence. The contents of this book are based on my personal observations and experience.

Where we came from and where we are going are difficult questions to contemplate in our modern day rush for financial survival. That bedlam between the Corn Flakes and the six o'clock news does not provide much time for concerted thought. It takes time - quiet time, and lots of it. It requires instruction, explanation and education on a subject which is the antithesis of materialism. One that is totally intangible, incomprehensible - another world - literally another world.

As logical human beings we require proof before we believe. I, for most of my life, accepted only what I could see, feel, eat or put into a cash register as real. I was the ultimate sceptic. On that memorable day in January '96 when I first squatted on the floor of the main hall at Abadiania, so close I could touch the action, armed with SLR camera and flash, I watched earnestly for the "hidden card", the slight of hand or the obvious set up. What I saw astounded me as it astounds countless thousands of first timers; I saw Raul, the subject of Chapter 1, rise from his wheelchair after 50 years as a paraplegic and walk. Still reeling from disbelief, my incredulity received a coup-de-grace when I witnessed a tumour removal from a woman's eye by a blindfolded Joao, using only a kitchen knife.

Now, having observed countless operations, healings and cures, including my own affliction, I am converting those energies I wasted on scepticism and false sophistication to this simple chronical of a man's dedication to humanity, on a scale and sincerity that defies our western logic. We all need proof as a means of verification but sometimes, even when we see the evidence, we still find it difficult to accept because its comprehension is contrary to our western upbringing. Such is the situation with the cures of Joao Teixeira da Faria.

Joao is a humble man who has a twofold purpose in life - to heal the sick and to make people aware that we are here on Earth to improve our level on the "other side". To elevate and better the position of our souls in the hereafter by what we do in this physical life.

Although he is probably the most observed, recorded and tested healing medium ever to enter this physical world, it is difficult for even the most dedicated author to compile a logical record of his life. Information about his early life is scant. As a youth he was more occupied with daily survival than recording dates and occurrences. Even simple chronological compilation of events in correct years of occurrence is a frustrating endeavour. There are no records save those in the memories of his associates, and they differ widely.

Joao himself is a poor source of precise details because he remembers nothing of his actions whilst incorporated by spirit and even when he is disincorporated he is still partially under their controlling guidance. Mediums of high elevation are, for the most part, attuned to spirit levels all the time (much like a television left ON with the volume turned LOW; they can still function but their attention is diverted).

Even today, his works are a fast succession of miracles, performed so quickly and in such frequency it is almost impossible to record the details of one before another is under way. The sheer numbers of people who seek his help allows little time for reflection or maintenance of precise records. He operates and treats more people in one day than a large western hospital achieves in a month. His staff are all volunteers, only one of which is dedicated to administrative records two days each week. That this book has been written at all is a miracle in itself; compiled from hundreds of newspaper articles, painstakingly translated from Portuguese, videos, discussions, interviews and frequent trips to Abadiania for first hand observations.

And so, to the issue of proof: we humans are strange creatures - sometimes we see the evidence but reject the explanation, grappling instead for our own to fit with our narrow, limited knowledge, preferably an explanation that isn't going to rock our conscience boat too much and one that does not require too much in the way of a radical life change. One that does not crack the protective shell of our understanding and perception. In light of the evidence in this book there is no alternate explanation.

Joao Teixeira da Faria is the living proof. He has been tested and examined by the best scientific minds this planet can muster. He permits and welcomes these investigations in the hope that they will prove to everyone the existence of the spirit world and the importance of living correctly in this life so as to elevate ourselves in the next, instead of enduring the choice of another reincarnation with the inevitability of consequences implied in the Laws of Cause and Effect, commonly known as karma.

Joao dedicates his life to healing the sick and incurable without payment and without prejudice. He encourages the video recording of his daily work and welcomes the observation of anyone, especially medical doctors whose participation he particularly welcomes. To see Joao pass his hand over the cancerous breast of a woman who has been diagnosed with malignant carcinoma and then lift her blouse to reveal a fresh incision, neatly stitched, and the tumour gone requires even the most reluctant observer to ask, "who did that?" The answer to this question is connected to the one we ask ourselves on those dark quiet nights, "what's it all about?" Perhaps the life story of this extraordinary man will help you find the answers to those questions.

# Introduction

Joao Teixeira Da Faria is arguably the most powerful medium alive at this time and must surely rank amongst the greatest of the past 2000 years.

A medium, as defined by the Oxford Dictionary, is a person *who is a spiritual intermediary between the living and the dead.* Joao not only communicates with spirit, he *incorporates* the spirit entity. He is literally *taken over* by the spirit and in so doing, looses consciousness, waking a few hours later without any knowledge of his actions during the incorporation. Whilst *in entity* his body is used as a means of conducting physical surgery and seemingly miraculous healing of the sick by the spirit entities who work through him.

His "gift" is not hereditary, it is not a learned technique, nor is it transferable to any other person. At the age of sixteen he accepted the responsibility of devoting his life to spirit incorporation for the purpose of healing the sick. He accepted a life-long task that would demand much of him and frequently repay him with abuse, personal deprivation, persecution and unlawful incarceration. To be trusted with such an awesome responsibility requires a strong, moral, righteous but humble man with unquestionable integrity. As if these restrictions and puritan criteria were not enough, he must also provide his service free of any charge to negate the criticisms of skeptics and to ensure that his divine gift is not denied. It is only in mid year 2000 that donation boxes appeared at the casa as a result of the devastating drop in the value of the Brazilian Real. This devaluation made it impossible for many Brazilians to travel to Abadiania so Joao and the Entities now travel to them. This has increased the costs of the casa considerably forcing the Entity approved decision to accept donations provided they are given freely without pressure.

To comprehend the enormity of his gift. To understand the amazing and true occurrences barely outlined in this book you must accept, albeit temporarily, the following beliefs:

1. *We have all lived many lives before this one.* We are incarnated and after this life we will be reincarnated again into another life. There are many well documented cases of hypnotists taking countless numbers of people back into past lives. They speak languages totally foreign to them and they describe in detail places and lifestyles of long ago which are frequently proven correct by subsequent investigation.

2. If you remove the physical shell we call the body what is left is the real you - your soul, your spirit consciousness. This eternal essence is in a perpetual state of improvement or decline, depending on what you do in each of your physical lives.

3. *Free will* is the only means by which the physical you, and subsequently your soul, can improve its position after your demise.

4. *Karma* is the means by which you choose pay your debt for wrongdoings or be enhanced for your free-will choice of good in each life. If you have killed, stolen, lied or cheated in a past life, chances are that you will be suffering some malady or conflict in your current life. Conversely, if you have been caring, considerate, honest and moral then your soul will have elevated and you will probably be a healthy well balanced person.

5. *There is a spirit world!* It is much more complex than our physical world. It is much more powerful and decidedly more beautiful for those who have earned an elevated place in it. It is multi level and multi dimensional to cater for the infinite number of development stages through which souls will pass. (Of over 150 Out-of-Body-Death NDE experiences surveyed by Kenneth Ring, author of *Heading Towards Omega: In Search of the meanings of Near-Death Experience,* New York: Quill, 1984

all reported similar observations, feelings and experiences to support this belief).

6. *Spirits, both good and bad, are with us all the time.* So many of those strange coincidences we experience, usually when we most earnestly wish for them, are the result of thought generation picked up by and acted upon by guides - *your* Spirit Guides. It adds real meaning to the biblical quotation *ask and ye shall receive.*

7. Our human bodies are generated from and protected by energy fields. There are seven corresponding layers each with its own density or frequency and seven major charkas (spinning vortexes). Some people can actually see these layers as Auras. If we live healthy, clean lives our energy fields protect us very well. Conversely, if we abuse ourselves with excesses of alcohol, drugs or unclean living the fields become weakened, will be attacked and attract undesirable attachments. Many diseases begin in these outer layers.

The mark of Joao's success is observable in the thousands who flock to his hospital style healing centre every Wednesday, Thursday and Friday. When he travels he heals as many as twenty five thousand in three days. The sick queue for hours, sometimes overnight, to see him. He never refuses anyone who is clean of heart and pure of intent. Although a devoutly God-loving man he accepts all without prejudice or religious bias. He heals the poor precisely the same as he heals the rich or famous. The world's elite seek his help when western medicine fails. Actress Shirley Maclean, congressmen, statesmen, priests, nuns, rabbi, the poor and the wealthy find their way to the small town of Abadiania in central Brazil to seek the help of Joao Teixeira Da Faria, known throughout Brazil as Joao de Deus (John of God).

To call him the "Miracle Man" is in a way a misnomer because a miracle implies the absence of a natural law when in fact his achievements are only the results of the law of reincarnation and the subsequent use of energies applied by spirit doctors from the spirit plane. He is classified as miraculous only because we in the western world are reluctant to accept that a spirit world exists and therefore that his work is the result of natural laws.

Of the hundreds of volunteers who give their time to the operation of the centre, most are grateful recipients of a new life after treatment by Joao and his spirit entities. Written off by medical doctors as incurable they found their way to Abadiania as a last resort. Amongst them are engineers, doctors, dentists, teachers, labourers, judges, civil authorities, businessmen and simple folk—there is no class division. They work in harmony to provide a loving and caring environment for those who, as they did, sought the help of Joao Teixeira Da Faria. These fortunate people put aside the restrictions of our modern thinking and dared to seek the impossible; to be rewarded, not only with a second chance at life, but a new understanding of their purpose in this physical world.

### Chapter 1

# The Man In A Wheelchair

Today was special for Raul Natal. Sitting in the wheelchair, which served as both his prison and his mobility for the past fifty years, he waited with apprehension and hope. He dare not raise his expectations too high, he had been to so many doctors and specialists over those long years. He had been X-rayed, tested, probed, manipulated and medicated without success until the doctors and he had finally resigned themselves to the fact that he would never walk again. Why would today be any different?

Raul heard about the healer, Joao Teixeira De Faria from friends. "He has cured hundreds of thousands of sick and crippled", they said. "Perhaps he could help you too." What did he have to loose? And so, in a final desperate pilgrimage, he endured the thirty six hour bus trip from Sao Paulo to the small town of Abadiania, high on the green plateaus of Goiaz state, in central Brazil.

It was 8.15am on a clear day blessed with the cool crispness of high mountain air. People seeking treatment, already five or six hundred, were packed into the main hall of the centre waiting quietly, each with their own thoughts and hopes as they watched for the healer Joao to appear. From his waiting position at the front of the crowd he saw the medium enter from a side door, hands clasped in front of his body, eyes intense. Joao took a middle aged woman by the hand and stood her against the wall. Rummaging through one of the instrument trays carried by a volunteer, he selected a common kitchen knife and began to skilfully scrape a tumour from her eye. Without anaesthetic or

19

sterilisation, using only the crude knife he scrapped away at the eyeball, a procedure which would normally cause excruciating pain and irreparable damage, but the woman showed no external discomfort. She remained calm standing against the wall without any observable reaction. Joao did not really seem to be concentrating. His hand swept the blade skilfully back and forth across the cornea but his eyes were focused out into the crowd, searching and scanning. It was as if someone or something other than he was removing the growth. In less than a minute he wiped the blade across her blouse and called to an assistant; "You can take her away. She is finished". Raul's mind raced in disbelief. His heart beat faster and his hands began to sweat. Could it be possible after all these years that he might walk again?

A man was led forward from the crowd and instructed to face the wall. He told the healer that he had not been able to sit or bend without pain for years. Gently Joao removed the man's shirt and, taking a scalpel, made a small one inch incision between his shoulder blades. Incredibly there was no bleeding and the man showed no sign of pain. "Lift your leg" said Joao. "Now bend over". Raul stared in disbelief as the man bent over and touched his toes. "Now squat down", said the healer and the man obliged effortlessly. The tears of relief and gratitude streaming down his face did not escape Raul's observation as the man was led away to the recovery room at the end of the hall. Raul's expectations were rising. Perhaps his dreams might yet be fulfilled.

Joao was already turning his attention to a woman with cancer of the stomach. He unbuttoned her blouse, slowly as if in trance, and lowered her waistband to expose her lower abdomen. From an assistant's tray he selected a scalpel and sskilfully made a small incision three centimetres long. It did not bleed and the woman seemed unperturbed. He cut deeper and inserted two fingers into the opening. Raul, from his front row position, saw the healer withdraw his fingers and with them a soft white growth the size of a golf ball. The woman remained motionless with no apparent discomfort. All of this, he noticed, was without anaesthetic or the stringent sterilisation of modern medical practices with which he was so familiar. The wound was stitched with a single suture and the woman led away to a small hospital style recovery room.

Another paraplegic in a wheelchair was now pushed forward. This would be indicative. If this man was healed there would certainly be hope for Raul. But when Joao told the helpers to wheel the man away to the Intensive Treatment Room, Raul's fragile confidence sank to an all time low. Perhaps it was too much to ask after all. No time to think now. Joao's voice jolted him back to reality.

"How long have you been paralysed?" Joao inquired in a deep compassionate voice.

"I have not walked for fifty years" replied Raul in little more than a whisper.

"What would you do if God gave you back your legs?" asked the medium. Raul was too stunned to answer. Short term confidence fought with years of despair. His mind raced. Could it be possible? Why would he ask if it were not? Surely it would be a cruel joke if he was not serious. He looked at the healer, his eyes were steady and he wore a confident, almost boyish smile. Raul wanted to speak but the words would not come. He knew his joints were seized from years of inactivity, they were calcified and immovable and his muscles atrophied.

> "In spiritual healing, the spirit intelligence (or guide) is not only able to obtain an accurate diagnosis of the patient's illness but is able to analyse the chemical substances causing the ill-condition, down to its molecular force designed to bring about a chemical change in that molecular structure for the patient's advantage." Harry Edwards, *A Guide to the Understanding and Practice of Spiritual Healing.*

21

"What would you do if God gave you back your legs?" asked Joao again interrupting his racing thoughts.

Raul did not know what to say he was still fighting with reason and logic. A kindly hand from behind touched his shoulder. "Answer him! How would you feel if you could walk again?" prompted the assistant.

All he could do was stutter. "I'd... be.. so very happy".

The healer bent down and briefly took hold of Raul's left ankle. As he did so a warm surge of life swept through the leg. "Now rotate it!" he said.raced. Could it be possible? Why would he ask if it were not? Surely it would be a cruel joke if he was not serious. He looked at the healer, his eyes were steady and he wore a confident, almost boyish smile. Raul wanted to speak but the words would not come. He knew his joints were seized from years of inactivity, they were calcified and immovable and his muscles atrophied.

"What would you do if God gave you back your legs?" asked Joao again interrupting his racing thoughts.

Raul did not know what to say he was still fighting with reason and logic. A kindly hand from behind touched his shoulder. "Answer him! How would you feel if you could walk again?" prompted the assistant.

All he could do was stutter. "I'd... be.. so very happy".

The healer bent down and briefly took hold of Raul's left ankle. As he did so a warm surge of life swept through the leg. "Now rotate it!" he said.

In spiritual healing, the spirit intelligence (or guide) is not only able to obtain an accurate diagnosis of the patient's illness but is able to analyse the chemical substances causing the ill-condition, down to its molecular force designed to bring about a chemical change in that molecular structure for the patient's advantage. HARRY EDWARDS *A Guide to the Understanding and Practice of Spiritual Healing.*

He obliged. It had been seized for as long as he could remember and now he was turning and twisting it! He watched in disbelief as Joao touched the other ankle and the same warmth engulfed it. It was like watching someone else's foot turning. It was unbelievable!

"Now," commanded the healer. "Stand up and walk!"

Raul froze."I can't!"

"Yes you can!" replied Joao with firm compassion; "Stand up and put this foot forward", he said pointing to the right foot.

With all his will and strength Raul lunged forward from the chair. His legs held – shaking, but they held. Joao extended his hand offering minimal support as he took his first steps in fifty years. His heart was beating so fast he feared it would seize. The happiness and relief were too much for him. An uncontrollable flood of tears poured down his face. He was walking!

Assistants led him away slowly to the main operation room where he sat on a bench with another twenty or so patients. A kindly man, dressed in white, with silver hair talked to them all of faith and love and how the healings were not the most important gift here. A greater gift is the awakening. The realisation that there is a life after death and that this physical life is just an opportunity for each of us to improve and elevate our soul. The healings were just a physical demonstration that we could see and experience but more importantly we must remember that the 'miracles' are performed by spirit entities who use the medium Joao Teireixa Da Faria as a vessel to perform their work[1].

> Six months later, in July 1996, Raul is walking normally. He has gained weight and his once atrophied limbs are stronger. He dedicates much of his time to assistance in the house - giving current, directing people with encouragement and helping out. If anyone says he looks good he replies: "Gracious o Deus e Joao" (Thanks to God and Joao).

---

1 Six months later, in July 1996, Raul is walking normally. He has gained weight and his once atrophied limbs are stronger. He dedicates much of his time to assistance in the house - giving current, directing people with encouragement and helping out. If anyone says he looks good, he replies "Gracious o Deus e Joao"

Raul listened and realised his life would not only be more active but more meaningful from this day on. Over the next six months Raul stayed long periods at the casa strengthening, striving, sometimes falling but steadily improving. Ultimately he was healed by the entities and the man they call John of God.

Whilst this type of instantaneous result is not unusual the greater percentage of people with long term physical maladies need time for the healing results to become evident. Spiritual healing creates change within body cells at a molecular level. The human body changes most of its cells over a period of approximately 180 days so the full results of healings can take a similar period of time or more even though some beneficial effects, such as the alleviation of pain, can be noticed soon after treatment.

Not infrequently the Entity will request a return visit because, following the cellular changes that will take place over the ensuing months, the body is bought to a new status before another treatment is warranted. In severe cases it may take an indeterminable time.

## Chapter 2

# The House Of Dom Inacio

They come in their thousands. The sick, the lame, the incurable and the medically discarded. Enduring long international flights and, for Brazilians living in the south of the country, gruelling thirty five hour bus trips to a small town high on the Goias plateau of central Brazil. Buses arrive all through the night. At 5am it is still. Along the road to the sanctuary the line of pousada, that cater for the thousands who pilgrimage here, is blanketed in a silent fog. People sit outside the simple lodging houses talking softly. There are not enough rooms to cater for them all so they sleep in cars or buses or simply stand around waiting for the dawn. The lodging houses provide free coffee for the weary travellers who spill from the newly arrived buses all through the night.

One hundred metres down the road the cluster of low white buildings is dark and silent. A kaleidoscope of stars forms a heavenly canopy above this Mecca of last hope -the place they call the Casa de Dom Inacio. Dawn will bring new light and with it new hope for a life without pain or illness for those who seek the help of Joao Teixeira.

The healing centre opens at 8am. The sick congregate to collect their queuing number. Cameramen prepare their equipment for filming of the day's activity. Somewhere in an unmarked room Joao rests and meditates alone in preparation for a day of healing. He will work until the last patient is attended to, sometimes if the people are many, far into the night. He lays on a simple couch in the semi darkened room. Above his head hang pictures of some of the entities including Dom Inacio, Christ and the Madonna. On the adjacent wall hang a dozen or more certificates of appreciation, they are but a few of the hundreds Joao has received for his work. Orders of government and honorary degrees bestowed upon him by grateful VIPs, governments and institutions. Amongst them is a Certificate of Honour from the President of Peru, in gratitude for healing his son. The basic furnishings reflect the simplicity of the man the people call John of God.

The centre resembles a small hospital. Painted stark white inside and out, with a sky blue band from floor to waist height. The design was supplied to Joao by his principal entity, Dom Inacio in a vision he received whilst walking through a small valley nearby. The centre, affectionately called The House, is named after this entity and is known in Brazil as Casa De Dom Inacio (The House of Saint Ignazio).

The choice of site is due to many things; the natural energy of this part of Brazil, the peace and quiet and because it is built on land rich in natural quartz which in itself provides a powerful energy source. Deep below there is a natural spring which flows to a small waterfall a kilometre away. Around this natural beauty grow many herbs similar to those used in the herbal mixtures prescribed by the entities. Situated on a high plateau, it looks out across the lush sweeping hills of Goias - a therapeutic sight in itself.

The location is one of intense energies, the understanding of which is almost beyond our physical comprehension. The best explanation comes from spirit itself, from a spirit called Seth, in information channelled by Jane Roberts in the 1970s. From her book *Seth Speaks. The Eternal Validity of the Soul*, Amber-Allen Publishing New World Library, comes the following explanation: "There are main co-ordinate points, sources of fantastic energy (which) represent accumulations of pure energy where health and vitality are strengthened. These points are like invisible power plants. They act as psychic generators, propelling what is not yet physical into physical form". Many believe the healing centre at Abadiania is one such location.

The house itself is designed around a central hall, open at one end leading out to a covered walkway, toilets and a rose garden. In this hall people congregate, waiting to witness the physical surgery by Joao-in-entity which occur twice each day. All of these operations are video taped by the house cameraman. Some years ago Joao requested the taping of the operations he performed "in entity" because he had no recollection of his actions once he incorporated the spirit. There are now thousands of hours of video records freely available to anyone at a modest charge to cover production costs.

In a semi circle around the hall are four principal rooms. The first is the recovery room, where patients are taken after treatment for care and observation until they are strong enough to leave. The effect of the anaesthetic, supplied by spirit, wears off in an hour or two and the patients are normally able to leave of their own accord without any visible side effects. The recovery room contains twelve single beds covered in clean white sheets. The nurses are all volunteers who provide compassionate care until the patients are able to leave.

Next door is the first of two "current rooms" fitted with rows of bench-style seats with a walkway through the middle. In this room, dressed in white, sit twenty to thirty mediums in meditation. This meditation provides the *current* to assist the entities in their work. (Interestingly, in the Edgar Casey readings on *Atlantis*, there is a reference to this type of combined energy used by the Atlantians to achieve their extraordinarily advanced civilisation - a similar production of spiritual current). The people who queue to consult with the entity file through this room first and as they do so they receive a spiritual "cleansing". In two corners there are piles of crutches, wheelchairs and body braces discarded by healed invalids - a silent monument to the success of the man and his entities in their healing work..

The second current room contains fifty or more mediums similarly seated in rows. The endless line of people pass through the middle and are spiritually prepared to meet Joao-in-entity who sits at the far end in a large chair covered in white linen. At the moment of meeting there is a split second recognition by the entity of each person's "blueprint"; their past lives, current situation, their illness and their spiritual awareness. Depending on what is seen, the person will be dealt with according to the requirement. Some are given herbal prescriptions. Some are told to return for surgery or treatment at a later time. A few are told to return next session as the Entity required for their case will be incorporated then. Those that need spiritual strength may be told to sit in current alongside those whose ailments are being treated whilst in meditation. Others are given concise instructions on necessary life changes. Each person is dealt with in less than twenty seconds. Herbal prescriptions are written at lightning speed in a spirit shorthand which looks like a squiggly line and a few ticks. The pharmacists of the house have been taught to understand these hieroglyphics by the entities who prescribe them.

The third room is the intensive operations room which has a dual purpose; very serious cases requiring a long time in curative coma and, those who request *invisible* operations. Around the wall is a line of single beds on which the intensive patients lay whilst the entities perform operations invisibly - paraplegics, leukaemia, AIDS and serious cancer patients. They may be in comma for a few hours or a few days depending on the extent of treatment required.

Across the middle of the room are rows of benches on which those requiring invisible operations sit, eyes closed, hands resting on their lap in meditation. No one should cross their legs or arms within the house, especially in current. A medium talks quietly to them explaining the procedure and raising their spiritual attunement. Twice a day Joao-in-entity will enter the room and declare, "In the name of Jesus Christ you are all operated. Let what needs to be done be done through me in the name of God". At this time all operations necessary are completed internally, without visible surface scars. (Scientific teams have found by X-rays, following these invisible operations, that there are often incisions and stitches internally. See Scientific Reports Chapter 8). In this room sit a number of special healing mediums.

Within the peripheral buildings that make up the remainder of the complex there is a commercial size kitchen where thousands of plates of soup and bread are served each day free of charge to those who come to the centre. Many have travelled thousands of miles and some are so poor they cannot afford to buy food. The house takes care of everybody in a like manner. There is a small coffee house, administrative offices, a large toilet block and a pharmacy for the preparation of herbal medicine. The whole cluster of buildings is contained within a fenced compound which provides parking for dozens of buses on one side and a shaded garden area on the other for quiet relaxation in the fresh mountain air.

### Procedures of the House

The centre opens at 7.30am each Wednesday, Thursday and Friday. At 8am people receive a short talk on the procedures and are asked to line up according to a number of criteria: first timers, second visit, revision or previously arranged operations. Those for operations are divided into visible or invisible. Those for invisible operation are taken to the intensive operations room for preparation. Those who request an visible operation are led to the main current room to meditate for half an hour before being taken to the main hall for their physical surgery. This will depend to some degree on which entity is incorporated as each has its own surgical specialities.

Joao meditates in a small private room at the rear of the complex before entering the main current room. To incorporate the spirit entity he simply stands before a table containing a simple wooden cross. He begins by asking that his hands be guided in the work of the day, then as he or an aide recites a simple prayer, the Entity enters him with a shudder of his great frame and takes control of his body. His relaxed slow movements and his campassionate gaze the only outward indications of the indwelling divine conciousness.

In mid 1998 Joao incorporated on the house stage in front of the waiting crowd. This was the first time he had incorporated publicly in more than twenty years. As a medium led the people in a quiet prayer, Joao stood motionless, eyes uplifted, hands clasped in front of his chest. In less than a minute his shoulders hunched forward, his head tilted back and from his open mouth an involuntary gasp of air rasped audibly across the room. Slowly gaining composure, his eyes focused into the audience - the Entity was back in this physical reality for another day's work.

Since that day Joao regularly incorporates publicly or in one of the current rooms simply by taking hold of a medium's hand, placing his hand on their head or their shoulder and drawing on their energy to assist the Entity across the boundaries of time/space. His eyes roll upward and a rasp of air heralds the arrival of the Entity.

After incorporation he takes the few who have requested physical operations by the hand and leads them to the main hall where he begins the visible surgeries. These surgeries are performed in front of the people waiting to consult the Entity.

Apart from the primary objective of alleviating the suffering of disease or maladies of the recipients, these demonstrations serve to prove the existence of the spirit world and the delivery of spirit healing through Christ energy. In addition they raise the level of belief and attunement within each person.

The healing and surgery is interspersed with asides to people in the audience as the entity sees, or reads, the blueprint of each individual. Sometimes with spiritual advice, or a suggestion to change eating habits or even a stern warning to change immoral behaviour. Often he will point to someone and direct them to go and sit *in current*. This could be for the healing benefits of the energy or because the person needs to meditate and raise their spiritual awareness before healing, or it could be because the person is recognised as a medium capable of generating powerful current. All of these events are videotaped by the house cameraman and may be purchased for a modest cost to cover production. They provide a valuable record of the achievements of the house and a souvenir for the recipient of the cure.

> "...all strength, all healing of every nature is the changing of the vibrations within, the attuning of the divine within the living tissue of a body to Creative Energies. This alone is healing. Whether it is accomplished by the use of drugs (herbs) or the knife, it is the attuning of the atomic structure of the living cellular force to its spiritual heritage."
> *Edgar Cayce Reading (1967-7).*

Joao-in-entity begins each session in the intensive operations room where he separates and prepares those who wish to be operated on physically. After he takes them out to the hall for their visible operations he returns to the rows of people seated in meditation for invisible operations. In one divine statement he calls for the operations to be completed. Some recipients feel the operations others do not but they are all completed immediately. Joao-in-entity then returns to the main current room where he sits to receive the people seeking consultation as they file past him one by one.

He dispenses with each person in an amazingly fast manner. As they approach, the entity instantly scans the body and is already prepared to provide the necessary advice. Some are given a prescription for herbal medicine, some are directed to the seats nearby to give or receive current, whilst others are directed to the invisible operations room for a spiritual passe or, if their surgery requires a different entity, they will be told when to return for treatment. He will remain until the last person is attended to.

At the end of the daily program Joao-in-entity will individually receive each of the mediums, who have sat for many hours providing current, for a blessing and to attend to any special requests they may have. He then stands up, begins a small prayer and the entity leaves his body with a visible slump.

### Follow the Rules.

As in every facet of life, there are rules to be followed. If the rules are broken, the treatment is impaired. This warning is delivered frequently by the house aides and Joao-in-entity, sometimes quite sternly if someone has come back for further treatment after disregarding the instructions.

It is not surprising, though that some people treat the rules lightly, they do not seem logical to our physical reasoning - another example of man's lack of understanding and the superiority of spirit knowledge. Some seem strange indeed; firstly there is a diet to be followed while ever herbs are being taken: *No pork, chillies, fertilized eggs, gassed banana or alcohol.* Why? Pork is a spiritually unclean meat. Chilli inflames the system. Fertilized eggs, when ingested, interfere with the healing effects of the herbs and treatments. Bananas chemically gassed are causing interference in the same way and alcohol disrupts the healing processes of the body.

Perhaps the most difficult to understand is the *No Sex Rule:* following an operation, visible or invisible, there is to be no sex for *forty days!* The explanation, that the energies of the body are in a healing phase and must not be disturbed by the physical energies of sex, does little to encourage people, now experiencing renewed health, to show restraint.

"As long as there is hate, malice, injustice - those things which are at variance to patience, long suffering, brotherly love - there cannot be a healing of this body. What would it be healed for? That it might gratify its own physical desires and appetites? That it might add to its own selfishness? If so, it had better remain where it is!" Edgar Cayce, *From one of his life readings of a man stricken with multiplesclerosis, restrained from recovery by his own bitterness and self pity.*

Of all the frustrations Joao and the entities endure, the most frequently encountered are those to do with disrespect for entities and their work and adherence to the simple rules for recovery. Every day, before each session, a member of the house provides instruction on this and other subjects in which it is stressed that these rules be strictly adhered to.

To disobey the instructions will result in a cessation of the healing process, a return to the pre-treatment condition or a worsening of the ailment, depending on the type of illness or infliction.

Whilst it is not a rule per se, there is a phenomena which should be remembered in case it should occur: if a patient, after returning home or to their hotel following an operation, faints they should be left alone and not moved for a few minutes. It may be the entity completing an operation. This can happen up to two or three days after the original operation. There is no cause for alarm but a phone call to the house will bring verification from Joao.

### Look, Learn and Change

Even the most casual or sceptical observer cannot help but be moved by the scenes of relief and compassion that exists everywhere in this small cluster of buildings.

> "To be sure the attitudes oft influence the physical condition of the body. No one can hate his neighbour and not have stomach or liver trouble. One cannot be jealous and allow anger of same and not have upset digestion or heart disorder." Edgar Cayce

Amongst the thousands who wait in line for hours, one can see an example of almost every type of human suffering. Pain and disease are the daily reality of those who suffer from them. Such people know and live with this intensely horrible reality. Many of them come because they are literally, practically, objectively hopeless. Modern medicine has given them up; in some cases the best specialists in the world. So where do they turn when all else fails?

Despite the hopelessness of their condition they all share a common look - their eyes carry the soft light of hope. When they emerge from their interviews, that hope has changed to happiness; a mother weeps for the cure of her small child, a cripple who could not walk gently coaxes his limbs to new found life with the caring aid of staff or friends. Everywhere there can be seen new hope, renewed life and a bond of love and caring for one's fellow man.

The true essence of charity can be seen everywhere; an old man shuffles up to the dispensary window fumbling his pockets for small change to buy his herbs. A kindly lady, realising his predicament, slips a fifty Real note into his hand. The small change will buy his bus ticket back home.

No wonder people come to simply observe, it is a moving and rewarding experience. Unlike many "miraculous locations" in other parts of the world there is none of the faith-healing aspects or mysticism of prophetic disciplines. *At Abadiania each person talks personally to the Entity and, following treatment, the overwhelming majority of them improve or are progressively healed.*

NOTE: Not everyone is cured in just one visit. Many things influence the recovery rate; time for tisuues to heal and cells to regenerate and nearly everyone needs to change spiritually. Some have to improve their environment, diet or way of life, others their attitude to their fellow man and to themselves. Whilst the majority of people are free to return home after treatment, it is not unusual for the Entity to request a return visit or to advise the patient to stay on for extended treatment.

"...all strength, all healing of every nature is the changing of the vibrations within, the attuning of the divine within the living tissue of a body to Creative Energies. This alone is healing. Whether it is accomplished by the use of drugs (herbs) or the knife, it is the attuning of the atomic structure of the living cellular force to its spiritual heritage." *Edgar Cayce Reading (1967-7).* In the first few months of year 2000 the Brazilian government devalued Brazil's currency by approximately 60%. The cost of petrol increased nearly 100% in less than six months. Thus the cost of travel internally has almost doubled and has resulted in diminished numbers at the house. Consequently, Joao established sub-centres in distant locations such as Rio de Janeiro, Vitoria and Rio Grande de Sul. He periodically flies to each of these centres between the weekly sessions at Abadiania. As a result there are far less people seeking treatment at Abadiania each day. The pousadas are not as full and, except on special occasions, there is ample accommodation available. To simplify the logistics of transporting bulky liquid herbs over vast distances, the entities gave instructions on how to prepare dry herbal medicines that are dispensed in lightweight plastic bags. As a result, the waiting time at Abadiania has greatly diminished and the Entity is not so pressed for time during consultation.

## Chapter 3
## Self-Operation

*"Our remedies oft in ourselves do lie, which we ascribe to heaven!"*
Shakespeare. All's Well That End's Well (1602-03).

The house had been operating for almost ten years. Joao had committed himself to healing the sick on three set days of the week; Wednesday, Thursday and Friday. Not because the entities were restricted by time but because they recognised the need for Joao and his patients to work within physical time frames.

Although Abadiania is situated in a remote area of central Brazil, people were finding their way to the centre adequately. Special buses were being hired to bring the sick from ever increasing distances; Sao Paulo, Rio de Janeiro, Vitoria and Bahia.

Things were beginning to stabilise in the house; the authorities closed their eyes to the miracles that were being performed and the reputation of the house was growing as each healed patient returned home to spread the word. At about this time too, the media was turning its attention to a young healer from Abadiania who seemed to be filling the void left by the popular healer Ze Arigo who died tragically in 1971 from a motor car accident when Joao was only twenty nine years old and the house was only a dream he shared with his guides.

Now, with the house operating regularly, his fame spread as the media reported the steady stream of miraculous healings with enthusiasm and increasing frequency. The work of the house grew as the numbers of sick multiplied and his supporters gathered for the privilege of working with him and for the enlightenment such work gave them. Just when he seemed to be fulfilling his destiny, disaster struck. Joao suffered a massive stroke. He was working in Bele Horizonte when he began to feel sick. Accompanied by his wife and devout supporters he was rushed to Belo Horizonte Hospital where he was admitted for examination.

It is normal medical practice to administer a series of tests to determine where in the brain the blockage has occurred; special X-rays, CT scans, magnetic resonance imaging, electronic measurement of the brain waves, blood tests and tests of the brain fluids in preparation for surgery to remove the obstruction of blood flow to the brain. But just as the tests began all of the equipment fused! Repairs were hurriedly carried out and the tests resumed, but again the equipment mysteriously burned out. The doctors administered sedation to Joao in preparation for surgery but, whilst they were preparing for the operation, Joao slipped out of the hospital and, accompanied by his entities, went home.

The prognosis however was not good; the stroke left him paralysed down one side of his body. He leaned to one side, his hands were stiff and one eye was crooked. He was only forty five years old!

Despite the handicap he tried courageously to carry on with his healing work. When he had recovered enough he returned to his beloved centre and sought incorporation of his entities who, he hoped, would be able to manage some limited surgery with his handicapped body. To the amazement of his assistants and patients his body showed no ill effects while he was incorporated with spirit, but unfortunately after the entity left his paralysis returned.

Joao continued this duality of his body for some months but eventually the entities told him to operate on himself. Such an unusual event needed to be witnessed and who better to record it than the media. A date was set and the event took place in the house in full view of cameramen, supporters and waiting patients. Joao incorporated his beloved entities and sat on a low stool in front of the crowd. He selected a scalpel from the instrument tray, lifted his shirt and sliced across his chest just below the heart. The three centimetre incision bled only a little. He inserted two fingers into the cut and without any sign of discomfort, probed into the cavity. It took only a few minutes, a simple suture to close the incision and it was done.

> "...anthropologists have witnessed shamans performing ritual surgeries on their own bodies - with no evidence of pain or subsequent scarring." James Redfield & Carol Adrienne, *The Celestine Prophecy - An Ex-periental Guide.*

When the entity left Joao's body his followers were delighted to see him renewed without a sign of impediment.

## Chapter 4

# The Revelations And The Persecutions

There was nowhere to run. The police trapped him in a corner of the market place as he talked with a friend. Baton sticks thudded heaviy into his body and the boots found their mark despite his attempts to ward them off. This was not the first beating he had to endure but it was one of the most severe. His head pounded, his body ached and blood was pouring from somewhere on his head.

The beating and kicking continued as they dragged him down the street towards the police post. The cobble stones tore at his flesh and bruised his back. Hauled to his feet and thrust through the door, they left him semi conscious on the floor while they waited for the senior officer to come and lay charges against him. The charges would be false or, as so often happened, the result of a warrant of malpractice raised by a medical doctor, but this time would be different. Joao could feel himself slipping away, the room spun and images of the laughing police officers was the last vision he held as the entities incorporated.

As the senior officer entered the room he and all of the punishing constables began to feel the pain of the beating themselves. They moaned and limped and slumped to the floor in agony. The entities of Joao had witnessed one too many beatings of their chosen physical instrument. They had entered the medium's body and transferred the pain to the offenders. To cease their punishment they released him without any further attempt at incarceration. Joao regained consciousness to find himself outside sitting on the street.

Persecution had become a way of life for Joao Teixeira De Faria. Since he discovered his healing gift at the age of sixteen he had spent most of his young life travelling from city to city exchanging healings and prophecies for donations of food, clothing, shelter or money. Inevitably word would spread to a medical practitioner or a dentist who's complaint would bring the police swooping down on him. If he was lucky he would be simply run out of town but more often he would be charged with a variety of felonies, thrown in jail and, not infrequently, severely beaten.

Sometimes there was an ironic side to these events. On one occasion, whilst healing in a town plaza, he was arrested. The senior police officer on this occasion was a woman who asked, with a touch of cynicism, to have her fortune told. To her surprise, the medium revealed so many of her dark secrets with such detail and precision that she was forced to make a deal - his freedom in return for his solemn oath not to reveal the secrets of her indiscretions.

On a number of occasions his persecutors actually asked for his help. Such was the case of a baffling murder which took place in Goiannia. The police could not find any suspects so they called in Joao to help and, as usual, Joao showed patience and understanding to those who previously ridiculed him. Within two days the police raided premises in which the suspects were engaged in selling the goods of the murdered man.

> "So if your goal is to avoid pain and escape suffering, I would not advise you to seek higher levels of consciousness or spiritual evolution. First, you cannot achieve them without suffering, and second, insofar as you do achieve them, you are likely to be called upon to serve in ways more painful to you, or at least demanding of you, than you can possibly imagine." M. Scott Peck, *The Road Less Travelled.*

Such was the young life of one of the most remarkable mediums of the past two thousand years. Persecution, ridicule and abuse. Always only one step ahead of hunger, deprivation or incarceration. Constantly on the move but still determined to carry on his divine mission of healing his fellow man and making them aware of their true purpose in this life

He was born in the small town of Cachoeria Da Fuaca, 24 June 1942 in inland Goias. The son of a simple tailor, Jose' Nunes de Faria, his was a heritage of extreme poverty. The family often went hungry from the meagre income his father was able to generate. No doubt his parents wished for an education for their son but poverty and his rebellious nature prevented them from providing him with schooling beyond second grade. The situation was further exacerbated by the boy's strong, often uncooperative nature. During his brief attendance at the local school of Santa Terezinha, he first exhibited this rebellious and defiant independence which would toughen him enough to achieve his destiny against seemingly intolerable odds. His behaviour resulted in his expulsion from school. His parents persevered and enrolled him in the Evangelic College where his behaviour was tolerated for only six months. He left, at the school's request, and joined the family in the daily effort to survive by becoming an apprentice tailor to his father. He spent a total of just two years in school.

What caused this disrespect for institutional control? Could it be that he, like so many exceptional people, possessed an inner knowing, a wisdom that sees beyond the narrowness and restrictions that would try to keep them within the groove of socially expected behaviour? Whatever the reason for his rebelliousness one thing is clear; Joao would never have become one of the greatest healing vessels of our time if he did not have that spark of independence which fired his instincts of survival against overwhelming odds. In this regard he shared a similarly defiant character with his main entity Dom Inacio who, despite being born into excessive wealth and high Spanish nobility, was rebellious in the extreme.

Life in Brazil during the 1940s & 50s was extremely difficult. The country struggled to survive on the export of coffee and sugar. Without diverse industries the economy was at the whim of international agricultural prices and the government continued to amass an impossible international monetary debt. In these harsh times a small boy in a poor rural town was fortunate to eat even once a day. Education was a luxury his family could not afford, even if he was a dedicated scholar. In hindsight it seems he was to be kept uncluttered by a formal education, not as a prerequisite for a spiritual life, but seemingly to prevent him from absorbing obstructive and conflicting human teachings.

Joao's spiritual manifestations began at an early age. He continually prophesied events to his parents and friends, events which would later be reported in the media. One particularly prominent prophesy occurred on a clear calm day as he was walking with his mother at a place called New Bridge. They were on their way to visit his brother. "Mamai", he said as they trudged along the dusty road. "There is going to be a big storm. Let's hurry." His mother disagreed pointing to the clear blue sky above.

"Yes Mamai! Believe me it is going to storm. I see many houses being swept away and people drowning. Please hurry", he insisted as he pulled on her arm.

They arrived at the village just as the violent storm broke. It rained and blew ferociously as they huddled in the shelter of a house at the edge of town. When it had subsided many people had been killed and twenty or more houses swept away, including the house of his brother.

Despite his prophesies he had no real understanding of spiritualism until the age of sixteen when a most remarkable thing happened. He had left Itapaci for Campo Grande to establish a tailor's shop, an enterprise doomed to fail for no one wanted suits during that particularly hot summer. Disheartened but driven by a need to survive he changed his profession to potter, making water barrels. This new vocation too was short lived and he was left with his constant companion, hunger. A few days later he was to experience a phenomenon that would change his life forever.

### *The Vision and The Gift.*

Joao had managed to find a job as a tailor near Campo Grande and began his first day at 0700. By noon his employment was terminated and he found himself out on the street with the old frustrations of joblessness and despair. It was a warm sunny day as the bare-footed youth approached a bridge across a creek on the country road leading to Campo Grande. The urge to bathe in the cool sparking water was too inviting to resist. He scrambled nimbly down the embankment and plunged in, momentarily washing away his thoughts of employment and hunger. He thought he was dreaming when he heard the soft voice call his name. Wiping the water from his eyes he focused into the shade of the overhanging trees. To his surprise, there in the shadows stood a beautiful fair haired woman. "Joao," she said again sweetly, "come and talk with me."

"How do you know my name?" he asked in astonishment.

"I know many things, and there is much I must tell you. Come, sit here with me".

Joao stayed and talked to the beautiful woman for some hours. That night, back in Campo Grande, he realised the vision was of Saint Rita of Cassia, the patron saint of Brazil. He turned over in his mind the things she had told him and woke with many questions to ask her. He dressed quickly and hurried out to the creek to see if she was there. The woman did not appear but in the place where she stood was a sparkling beam of light. Disappointed he turned to go when he heard her voice. "Joao. You must go to the Redemptor Spiritual Centre in Campo

Grande. They are waiting for you there," she said as the light disappeared.

The youth began the long walk back to town, curious and perplexed. But just as the woman said, there was a man waiting for him at the door of the centre. "Please come in. We have been waiting for you" he said, as he took him by the arm. Joao does not remember the next three hours but when he woke up people surrounded him smiling and shaking his hand.

"You took on the entity of King Solomon. You healed many people and performed amazing operations" said the senior member.

"I what?" replied Joao in disbelief. "I'm sorry, you are mistaken. I was just hungry and fainted from the need of food."

"Let us go to my house and prepare some food. He is starving!" instructed the senior.

Bathed, dressed in clean clothes and sitting at a table laden with a sumptuous meal Joao had time to reflect on the claims of the people around him. It was time to take his gifts more seriously; he was unaware of the life long burden this decision would make for him.

Joao stayed in Campo Grande for three months, healing the sick at the spiritual centre and receiving clothing, food and shelter in return. It was at this time that he was to receive his first real education in spiritualism from Master Yokaanon who awakened his awareness to the spirit world at the temple of Fraternity Electic Spiritualist Universal. He had already decided to accept the responsibility of his calling for the rest of his life, unaware of the price he would have to pay to fulfil the mission. But the basic necessities of life still needed to be satisfied within the young Joao so, a few months on, he set aside his spiritual learnings and continued his search for work. It was to be a long and painful road to his eventual destiny.

He left the spiritual centre and began work as a brick maker, carrying clay from the pit to the brick machines. Whether it was spirit intervention or just lack of physical capability is unknown, but he was unable to meet his quota each day and was eventually fired. It is ironic that thirty seven years later he practices as one of the greatest healers the world has ever known, directly across the road from a brick factory.

During his travels in search of work he gave healing and spiritual guidance where ever it was asked of him. His family disapproved and this conflict bought with it the first indication of the sacrifice he would be required to pay for his beliefs and his dedication to the suffering of others. Since those early days he has lost count of the persecutions, beatings and incarcerations he has had to endure to uphold those beliefs.

### *The Persecutions*

For almost eight years Joao lived the life of a vagabond. Moving from city to city in search of employment, healing the sick and instructing the ignorant of their spiritual obligations along the way. He could only stay in one place as long as he remained undiscovered. When the news spread about his amazing cures it was inevitable that a medical practitioner, dentist or even the local priest would take offence and bring the heavy hand of the law crashing down on him. Ultimately, fabricated charges would be laid and he would be thrown in jail. Upon release he would walk or beg a ride to a new city only to begin his quest again.

For some years he lived in the northern state of Bahia, where the population is predominately of black African origin whose ancestors were bought there as slaves to work the sugar cane fields. The slaves were subjected to horrendous cruelty by their masters, so they retaliated with their black spirit rituals Quimbamba

47

and Macumba which their ancestors bought from Africa. Here he was only able to carry on his work by disguising his healing in these rituals; meeting groups of people at clearings on the edge of town to provide them with cures and spiritual guidance.

Finally, after eight long and difficult years, he could not endure the persecutions any longer and sought refuge in the military barracks at Brasilia as a civilian tailor. In return for protection he healed the sick amongst the military personnel and their families, remaining under the protection of the army for nine years until eventually the entities insisted he could no longer limit himself to a privileged few. It is said that he made a pact with the entities; they would take care of his financial needs and he would dedicate himself to humanity. To this end he was instructed to use the small amount of money saved during his refuge in the military to buy a small fazenda. Farms in this area are not very productive to irregular rainfall but they are extraordinarily rich in minerals—his farm contained emeralds, enough to establish the beginnings of his centre in Abadiania, a place selected for him by spirit guidance through his clairvoyant friend Chico Xavier, and began his first permanent healing centre in a small building near the highway. He has been providing his services from this small town for the past twenty years, moving the centre to its present location in 1978.

## A Conflict of Law

Despite his amazing contribution to mankind in the alleviation of suffering, he is still pursued by the authorities, spurred along by disgruntled factions; those medical doctors who fail to understand the source of his healing and surgical ability calling on support of their medical associations to take action, and the church whose clergy fear a weakening of their position within the community and fail to recognise the same spiritual source that is the very core of their doctrines.

In 1981 a writ was issued against him for practising medicine illegally. The court session was held in Anapolis only twenty kilometres from his healing centre. Fortunately his work is so well known in the area that a huge groundswell of public support, including grateful legal practitioners, resulted in an acquittal.

The acquittal raised intense resentment amongst a minority group headed by a well known Anapolis doctor and political leader. On August 17, 1982 he arranged a serious attempt on Joao's life by four men in three cars. Although details are sketchy his survival was acclaimed as a miracle.

Even as this book goes to print there is an action in progress, prompted by the Regional Medical Council of Espirito Santo and pursued by the Public Prosecutor through the Brazilian Penal Code.

This latest challenge manifested early on the morning of 28th of March 1995. Three policemen arrived at a special healing session due to begin in the Floriano Varejas Exhibition Park in the city of Carpina. They entered the park, where 9000 people waited to see Joao, with a warrant for his arrest. He was saved only by the quick action of his lawyers, Jaques Pereira and Sabastiao Soares, who immediately filed for a Habeas Corpus to prevent the healer from being jailed. The lawyers wisely approached Supreme Court Judge Antonio Feu Rosa who directed District Judge Joao Miguel Filho to issue the Habeas Corpus. Judge Feu Rosa had received an operation from Joao (other eminent legal hierarchy who have sought the healing entities of Joao include Supreme Court Judge Jose de Oliveira Rosa and Minister of the Supreme Court, Justice Hilmar Gaivao).

In his book *The Phenomenon of Abadiania*, Supreme Court Judge, Jose Liberato Costa Povoa, argues strongly for the law to be intelligent about its interpretation, pointing out that several court cases had set a precedence which should be considered, particularly in their recognition that acts performed by *incorporated* entities were not crimes. He quotes from the case Tribunal de Alcada Criminal de Sao Paulo in which the eminent Judge Azevedo Junior states *"In the exercise of quackery the presence of fraud is presupposed, which cannot happen to the mediumized individual. This last, in a state of trance, finds himself unconscious and therefore may not be held responsible for actions undertaken in his absence by the spirits incorporated in him".*

Judge Povoa is scathing in his attack on his colleges, calling them hypocrites for penalising genuine healers who do so much good for the their fellow man, including the healing of magistrates, lawyers and judges. He slights them for their "lack of courage" in choosing not to recognise the strength of spiritual healing but "cling exaggeratedly to the letter of the law". He boldly points out that the law may be favourably interpreted if it is accepted that the cures are not carried out by the mediums themselves but by *"illuminated entities incorporated by them".* He quotes from another Federal Supreme Court Appeals; "State v Inacio Bittencourt" in which the eminent Minister Viveiros de Castro stated, in his review on 23 October 1923:

"I cannot call it a practice of medicine, if a cure is affected by natural means. I find that the procedure of the appealing party is not the practice of medicine, but the manifestation of a religious creed, worthy of the respect due to any other religious creed.

*Now, I have not yet heard of anyone intending to bring to trial ecclesiastical (religious) authorities who perform miracles. To cure by means of Spiritism is to believe in a supernatural intervention. For these reasons, the fact must be considered in itself, not as a manifestation of belief".*

It is indeed a strange parody of justice that so many of the administrators of the law, which provides the lance to destroy the good works of Joao and his entities, should be grateful recipients of his gifts. However, the law is established to prevent charlatans from exploiting the public and should not in itself be condemned. The real culprits in this case are those factions of the community who, because of egotism and an imagined threat to their self erected status, choose to destroy rather than work with this humanitarian facility, and in those members of the legal fraternity who allow themselves to be persuaded by such factions to enforce the letter of the law when there is ample precedence to enable them to judge leniently in favour of genuine healers.

In any effort to bring down the house and its good works charges against Joao must be brought under one or more chapters of the labyrinthian Brazilian Penal Code. The laws in Brazil are patterned almost entirely on ancient Roman law, and they contain many ambiguities. The main articles under which he can be charged are 282 and 284; the illegal exercise of medicine and of healing. These articles show clearly that it is a crime to "exercise healing by prescribing, giving or applying any substance; using gestures, words or any other means and making diagnoses". The penalty for this infringement is imprisonment for six months to two years.

His lawyers, of course, could argue that he does not prescribe medicinal drugs, only herbs. That he applies no substances, and that any diagnosis is not made by him but by an incarnate spirit. As far as "using gestures, (or) words" could be considered a crime, it would mean that all churches in Brazil are also guilty. Priests and clergymen constantly make gestures in every prayer and service!

There is always such a ground swell of public support for the healer that it seems remarkable these factions should attempt to have him incarcerated, and yet technically, he is breaking the law. Prior to Joao's rise in prominence as an incorporated healer the now deceased Brazilian healer Ze Arigo was brought to trial under the same articles of the penal code. Although the public, the press and the bulk of the legal profession were solidly behind him, the law prevailed under the dour disposition of one Judge Marcio de Barros, and on March 26, 1957, Ze Arigo was sentenced to one year and three months jail. It was only through the intervention of the President of Brazil, Juscelino Kubitschek, who owed his life to Arigo and his entity Dr. Fritz, granting him a presidential pardon under Article 87, No 19 of the Constitution that he was freed after five months in prison.

What the outcome for Joao will be in the forthcoming court case is unknown. The paradox of a judgement deliberated by the highest judicial minds in the country, whilst publicly acknowledging their own personal experience of humanitarian relief so freely given by this man, albeit in defiance of the law, is a most unenviable situation. For Joao, however, the axe hangs over his head every day of his life while ever there are those factions, whose inflated sense of sophisticated professionalism, cause them to feel (unjustifiably) threatened.

Paradoxically, his persecutors not infrequently seek his help, either openly or clandestinely. On Wednesday 3 July 1996 one of Brazil's most persistent police prosecutors, Commissioner Firto Franki, silently joined the long line of people waiting to see the entity. The dark blue sacks under his eyes and his sallow complexion indicated severe kidney and liver problems. His body was showing the accumulation of incorrect living habits; excessive weight, difficult breathing and his downcast eyes carried the resignation of a very ill man.

The incorporated entity, Dr. Augusto De Almeida, recognised him instantly and the medium Joao rose from his chair. He pulled him to one side and, calling six people from the current, circled the lawman. "Please tell these men who you are." said the entity sternly. The policeman stated his rank and position in the force. "You have pursued me for more than ten years. You have made my life hell and now you come to me for help?! Let me show you, once and for all, the extent of my work." He turned to the six men and asked them to describe their own miraculous healings. The lawman listened to each with his head hanging low on his chest; three paraplegics, two terminal cancers and one doctor who was blinded by a motor car accident, all cured.

"You came to me ten years ago under false pretences of being ill and then testified against me as a fraud based on your own lies. You knew my work was authentic because you sent your friends to me for treatment, but still you continued to persecute me. Do you publicly acknowledge here before these witnesses that my work is genuine?"

The policeman, now chronically ill and exposed, hung his head and nodded. "Yes, I will give written testimony if you require it. I know you are not a fraud and I know what good works you have done for people." Joao resumed his seat and wrote a prescription to help the man who had persecuted him for more than a decade.

Joao survived the court case that was pending as this book went to print but there have been many more since. In early 2000 he faced a formidable challenge in the courts of Brasilia. The case against him looked so solid that he did not eat for three weeks. Ultimately the verdict was passed in his favour and another precedent set for possible protection in any future trials.

During the anxious weeks leading up to the trial date the entities performed no visible surgeries for fear of providing the prosecution with evidence against the medium Joao. A week after the decision was handed down the visible operations began again and Joao continued with his life mission.

## Chapter 5

# The Medium And The Entities

*Medium. adj. A person used as a spiritual intermediary between the dead and the living.* Collins English Dictionary.

### The Medium

Joao Teixeira Da Faria is a medium of extraordinary capabilities. His mediumship enables him to take on, or *incorporate*, thirty three entities, all of whom were remarkable people during their own physical lives. The entities are spirits of deceased doctors, surgeons, healers, psychologists and theologians who are of such high soul elevation they need no longer reincarnate to our physical plane. They do, however, continue to elevate in the spirit plane by the extent of their benevolence and charitable works. Using his body as a vessel they are able to perform miraculous operations and cures of the sick and the crippled. The thousands who flock to Abadiania for treatment each week and the number of people, who count in the millions, now living healthy lives offer irrefutable testimony to this theory and to the success of Joao and his entities.

The man Joao Teixeira is strong, decisive but paradoxically sensitive and totally dedicated. Not all mediums are possessed by their spirit guides but in this case he is completely taken over by spirit entity. He is an unconscious medium. His person becomes that if the incorporating entity. During an operation there is a trance-like serenity in both his eyes and his face. His fingers work with skilled precision, even when his head is turned or his attention is diverted elsewhere. Many of the surgical routines cannot be done even by highly skilled surgeons. Unincorporated, he admits he knows nothing of medicine, cannot stand the sight of blood and hates injections.

His patients, without any preoperative preparation, are completely relaxed, calm and show no fear whatsoever. They remain impassive throughout, yet have received neither tranquillisers nor anaesthesia. There is no expression of pain, tension or anxiety. They don't even move. To the casual observer he seems to work in blatant defiance of medical precautions and yet there has never been a single case of septicaemia (blood poisoning) in over forty years of surgery.

Joao is a devoutly God-fearing man was raised in the Roman Catholic faith but follows no particular religion or creed. His entire purpose in living is the love and care of his fellow man through the alleviation of their suffering as directed by his spirit guides. Spirtual healing mediums generally are devout believers in Christ and seem to embrace the Spiritist theories of Allen Kardec, (1803 - 1869) a French author and medium, who developed the principals of communication between the physical and spiritual worlds. One of his tenets said: *"The spiritual world is in constant contact with the material world, each reacting with the other. This is what the spirits themselves have dictated"*. He wrote that science and religion were not in conflict with each other. *"Science was revealing the laws of God but science had a great deal more to learn - particularly in regard to the paranormal."* Kardecists believe that the spirit world is less condensed than the material world, but *"it is the primary world of reality, and the material world is subservient to it"*. They believe too that some trance mediums are able to incorporate entities from the spirit world - a case of benign possession. In the case of Joao his body and mind are literally "taken over" by the entity who supplies the diagnostic and surgical knowledge necessary for the patient being treated. He is possibly the finest example of a full trance medium living at this time.

It is not Joao's hands performing the operation nor his mind that prescribes the herbal medicines. He has little or no memory of what takes place - an amnestic veil descends upon him for the full duration of the incorporation. In his own words: "It is not me who cures. God is the healer - I am simply the vessel".

### *Invisible and Simultaneous Operations.*

Joao is capable of incorporating only one entity at a time, although he can change entity at any time as the need arises, and it does not preclude any number of entities performing operations at the same time outside of his body. These are called *simultaneous* operations and occur without notice during the physical operations in public view, patients in the crowd are operated on by the accompanying spirits without warning. They simply faint from the spirit anaesthesia and are carried away to the recovery room by assistants. It is recorded that over seventy of these simultaneous operations occurred in just one day!

*Invisible operations* are those which leave no external sign of entry into the body. The operation occurs internally. Subsequent X-rays frequently show the internal incision and sutures but there are no external marks.

Most of the healings performed by Joao are invisible or instantaneous but each day there are two public demonstrations of physical surgery, *visible operations*, specifically performed to enable people to "see" the entities at work. This is done to fulfil the centre's mission of, not only healing the sick, but providing irrefutable proof that there is another dimension - a spirit world, where we all eventually go when this physical life expires.

## Spirit Anaesthesia and Antisepsis.

There are many energies and much knowledge available to the spirit entities which we in the physical world cannot comprehend. Some of these, or the results thereof, are observable in the public demonstrations; anaesthesia, antisepsis and minimal blood loss are some of the more amazing, as are the techniques used.

Anaesthesia is supplied by forces from the spirit dimension, an invisible power, a magnetism or numbing energy emanating from Joao's presence and particularly from his hands. The patients simply stand or sit in total oblivion to the surgical procedure. There is an absence of pain or discomfort for what, under normal conditions, would be literally unbearable. There is a mild after effect of the anaesthesia so patients are carried away to a recovery room until the effects have worn off, normally in an hour or two.

Antisepsis is also supplied invisibly. As a demonstration, Joao will often dip a cotton swab into a bowl of water and touch it to the lips of an observer, preferably a medical practitioner if one is available. The lips, as reported by all who experience it, feel numb for some hours afterwards and yet the water is drinkable. There has never been a known case of infection in the house even after hundreds of thousands of physical operations over the past forty years.

In modern medical procedure it is normal practice to administer strong antibiotics immediately after surgery - this is not the case with entity operations, in fact, antibiotics are not recommended because of their anti-life side effects. Herbs, however, are often prescribed. The recovery and operation rooms have a distinctly sterile odour, not the pungent smell of known antiseptics so prevalent in modern hospitals but rather a light, cool freshness clearly noticeable to the aware observer.

Minimal blood loss is another observable phenomenon. Barely a trickle is seen from even the largest incision and is quite baffling to surgeons who understand how difficult it can be to check the flow of blood without cauterising blood vessels.

It is not uncommon in Brazil for medical doctors to call on mediums for diagnostic and treatment information. In Sao Paulo a group of physicians and surgeons, many of whom were trained in the USA, regularly consult with in-house mediums. The mediums are able to draw on the skills and knowledge of doctors in the spirit world for information not available in our physical world. There is even a hospital which operates with this co-operation on a daily basis.

To be a medium of the calibre of Joao Teixeira Da Faria - to be entrusted with the awesome responsibilities of healing the sick requires a very special person, one whose soul has developed to a high level and one who, in the physical world, has unquestionable integrity and morals. Common amongst most healing mediums is a strong presence, or magnetism, an unusual physical strength and an unshakable belief in their destiny and purpose. This is certainly the case with Joao who is a heavily built man with a remarkably strong presence and yet this individuality and strength of purpose exists in harmony with his obvious humility and unswerving dedication to his mission.

Whilst there are many spiritually aware educated intellectuals, including medical practitioners, it seems peculiar that a person so uncluttered by education and the burden of proof absolute required by modern science, should be given the "gift". Ze Arigo, the famous Brazilian healer who died in January 1971, was also a simple man. Joao, with only two years primary schooling, is "uncluttered" in the extreme. It seems the spirits might prefer it that way, perhaps avoiding a conflict between the somewhat learned rigidity of an educated mind and the intangible concepts of spiritualism.

### The Entity Knows Everything

For some people it is difficult to comprehend the extent of spirit capabilities, to accept that there is an existence where there is no time and no space, that spirits have access to energies and knowledge that we in the physical form disbelieve or at best consider as supernatural. To understand that spirit knows everything, knows a person's thoughts and be able to read a blueprint of their soul, their past lives, their karma, their intentions and their current activities, good or bad. Joao-in-entity reads each person's "blueprint" as they appear before him, instantly scanning their body for medical problems. He is also alerted by this spirit 'knowing' to any unscrupulous or indecent intentions in the house.

One example of this phenomenon occurred in the house in February 1996. Joao-in-entity sat in the healing chair receiving a long line of people wanting consultation. He had incorporated a principal entity, Dr Oswaldo Cruz, a spirit who still displays the strict disciplined personality of his physical life.

He summoned a member of the house and said: "There are three men sitting outside in the main hall. Tell the one in the blue floral shirt to leave the premises. He is not welcome here". Later it was revealed that the man was married, had two mistresses and lived a deceitful and selfish life. The entity knew that his purpose at the house was not a moral one and dispatched the bewildered man before he could line up for counselling.

A woman, who had been to see him two months prior, complained that the herbs she had taken for her sick friend had no effect as she was still ill. "Did she take the herbs?" asked Joao. She, of course, replied in the affirmative. "I am sorry my child, she did not. I cannot help your friend if she pours the herbs down the sink". The woman stared open mouthed and meekly accepted the new prescription without another word.

On another occasion Joao-in-entity, was conducting physical operations before a large crowd in the main hall. As he completed an operation he turned to a middle-aged TV cameraman who was recording the proceedings and said: "You, with the camera! You are not a good man! You are dabbling in the wrong things. You know what I am talking about don't you!?" The man lowered his camera and nodded in stunned amazement. "You must change your ways or suffer the consequences of a heavy karmic debt. And look at you, you are not caring for yourself. Too much alcohol, smoking and wrong lifestyle. I'm sorry but you need to be told". With that Joao turned to the next patient and continued operating leaving a sweating red faced cameraman.

There are many recorded times when the entity has had to talk to the Children of the House, as the helpers are affectionately known. One such occasion was when a highly valued medium, seventy four year old Donna Ilva, who travelled 2400 km every fortnight to provide spiritual current, was refused service by a kitchen worker who falsely accused her of pushing in. Despite the support of those around her she was obliged to return to the end of the line. When the proceedings began again after lunch Joao-in-entity called for all the staff to assemble in the hall; "My children there is some lack of respect for our valued people in the house", the Entity said looking directly at the medium. "We are all children of the Light and we cannot tolerate petty prejudices from anyone". This he directed at the kitchen worker. "Let us have no more of this. Love one another as you love yourself".

Perhaps the most dramatic and tragic example of the entity's ability to see and know all was the warning to Joao about his nephew. On Sunday 25th February 1996 his nephew was due to fly his private plane to Joao's property near Anapolis for a lunch time meeting. The medium woke at dawn and, despite the early hour, phoned his nephew insisting that he did not fly that day. The entity had warned Joao that he would crash if he did. The nephew, a proficient but sometimes careless stunt pilot, laughed and hung up, content in his assumption that the entities would protect him. The medium phoned again and begged him not to fly. Unfortunately he disregarded the warnings and crashed on landing at the farm strip, watched by Joao and his family. The plane hit a power line on approach and erupted in a ball of flame. Not only did the centre lose its head pharmacist, Joao lost a very close friend and beloved relative. He was so distraught he could not provide a service at the centre. Thousands were turned away and his followers wept for his sorrow.

### The Entities.

Spirit entities who use Joao for healing works were all exceptional people during their last incarnations to the physical world. During incorporation each entity carries with him his own personality from the past life and, to those who work in the house regularly, each one can be recognised in Joao's behaviour. It has been recorded by investigating scientists that even the colour of his eyes changes to match the colour that particular entity had when alive.

The first incorporation by Joao, when he was sixteen, was the spirit of King Solomon. He is still working with him today a reminder that, unlike humans, the spirit is immortal unfettered by time and space.

The principal entity is that of Dom Inacio De Loyola, after whom the house is named. This Spanish nobleman was born in 1491 into one of the richest families in Spain. His violent and aggressive nature served him well as an officer in the Spanish army against the French at Navarra where he was wounded in the leg and, along with his men, was captured. His valour earned the respect of the French and secured freedom for himself and his soldiers. His leg required an operation from which he was not expected to recover. During three days of comma he received a vision of the Apostle Paul. The vision prompted him to change his ways, to study the teachings of Christ and compare his self indulgent ways to that of Jesus. After months of painful convalescence, during which he studied and wrote, he began turning to a new way of life.

A few weeks after discharge a vision of the Virgin Mary appeared and instructed him to travel and teach the way of the Light. He gave away all of his possessions, left his family and journeyed throughout Spain preaching his version of the gospel. He lived the life of a beggar, was ridiculed and persecuted and eventually became gravely ill. During eight days of comma in hospital, without food or movement, he saw many visions of spirits who encouraged him to continue. He recovered and in 1524 pilgrimaged to Bethlehem to continue his studies. When he returned to Bacelona he established the order of Jesuites, a religious faction contrary to the ruling Roman Catholic Church. It was the time of the Spanish Inquisition and his teachings were not appreciated by the wardens of the church. Arrested for heresy, thrown into a dungeon with murderers and criminals his suffering only toughened his resolve. Following his eventual release he was prohibited from teaching religion in Spain so he travelled to Paris and then to Holland where, in 1534, he established another order. Despite constant persecution he gathered a large following through his spiritual guidance and healing with the laying-on-of-hands. Finally he moved to Rome where he gathered another large following under the new order, eventually growing so strong that, in 1540, he was recognised by the Pope. He travelled to Brazil to spread the good works of the Jesuites but fell ill there and was forced to return to Rome where he died in 1556.

The Casa de Dom Inacio is so called because of the similarities between the life of this entity and the life of Joao. Both were lives of constant persecution, incarceration and ridicule. Both teachings maintain a simple spiritual philosophy based on early religions; a belief in the love of God (as opposed to the fear of God), Christ, Holy Spirit and reincarnation but uncluttered by modern religious dogma and self interest.

When Joao incorporates the entity of Dom Inacio he exhibits calm, patience and paternity. His unlimited compassion is distinctly observable and often causes tears and emotional reaction in the patient who receives his healing energy.

Oswaldo Cruz, another principal entity, was responsible for the eradication of Yellow Fever in Brazil and conducted scientific experiments for many endemic diseases. Later in life he assisted in the planning of Brazil's modern capital Brasilia. A direct and forthright man of controlled personal discipline, he exhibits a concise and disciplined character in Joao during incorporation. He is not beyond offering unsolicited advice to patients and observers if he sees an undisciplined character, much to the amazement of the recipient. When this entity is within Joao he requests that people remove all wristwatches because it disturbs his current.

Of Dr. Augusto de Almeida's last life there is little information but it is known that he was a general medical practitioner and surgeon who combined his spiritual awareness with his medical expertise in the treatment of his patients. His presence in-entity is identified by his gentle caring nature and strong authoritative personality. He is very serious about his work and his disciplinarian nature is observable in the extreme perfection of his surgery. He will rebuke anyone who disrespects his work, and any interruption during the treatment of a patient will bring a disapproving stare. One of the principle surgeons of the house, his total concern and concentration is dedicated to the patient.

Dr. Jose Valdivino is another precision surgeon about whom little is known. His presence is observable as extremely loving and caring with sincere attentiveness to his patient's ailments.

He is a father image to everybody in the house and is one of the main operating surgeons. He possesses an amazing energy which he uses for curing paraplegics in a truly miraculous manner, sometimes with just a touch of his hand and a command for them to rise and walk.

Other principle entities include King Solomon and Dom Ingrid, an extraordinarily powerful entity about whom nothing is known except that her energy is so strong that she will make Joao's nose bleed if she comes too close to him. Of the thirty six entities many do not wish to reveal their identities but they are all highly specialised in their particular field; orthodontists, lawyers, theologians, chiropractors, dentists and herbalists. Each provides their specialist advice as and when required.

### The Medium-in-Entity

To observe Joao in entity is a profound experience. One who is remembered by all that observe him. His friendly boyish face changes from a soft alert demeanour to a deep compassionate calmness. When he stares unblinking into the faces of those who seek his help it seems he is looking into their very soul—many begin to cry unexplainably. There is a divine reverence about him that people respect and revere and yet he does not demand reverence from anyone.

There is a Godliness about him that escapes no one. He seems to radiate light and energy that can be felt by all. Many say that this is the greatest healing of all—the healing of the soul.

No one is ever quite the same after observing Joao-in-entity, their lives are changed forever and they take away with them an inner peace that cannot be described, only experienced. In time those that observe his works are at peace with themselves in the realization that they have seen God work through a remarkable vessel incarnate on Earth– a living saint in our time. Many agree his healings are Christ like and yet he is the first to say: "I do not heal. It is God that heals. I am just the vessel".

Those who have had the privilege to be in his presence and to receive his healing or his blessing are profoundly changed and go forward in life with an understanding of life and their part in it. The fear of death is replaced by a contentment in the knowledge that the passing will be easy and painless—they know they do not die but simply return home. This is a realization that comes when one observes a demonstration of the reality God's existence.

Joao often pauses during a visible operation and addresses the crowd telling them that he does not have to perform these physical operations. He points out that the entities perform them in order to raise the acceptance and belief of those who come for treatment. He could simply call on divine intervention of the spirit guides as he does during invisible operations. The problem is, who would believe him? "I do not have to do it this way. This is so you will believe." He instructs.

These days there are new entities arriving with faster and more amazing operations and cures. As they progress on the "other side" they seek to bring the new techniques to house. Many people fail to recognize this and are disappointed when Joao-in-entity simply waves his hand at one or more in the line and says; "It is done already. Just sit in the current".

### Chapter 6

# The Children Of the House

Unlike most mediums, Joao performs in a surrendered hypnotic trance and has no recollection of his actions whilst incorporated. Consequently he depends a great deal on the help of others to record his actions and the directions of the entities and to assist in the running of the house. The increasing numbers who seek his help place enormous strain on the tiny hospital and its facilities and it could not function efficiently without the dedication of volunteer staff, more than two hundred and fifty of them, affectionately called "The Children of the House" by Joao and the entities.

Most of the volunteers came with their own life-threatening ailments. In gratitude for a second chance at life they willingly dedicate whatever time they can afford to the function of the house as 'current' mediums, assistants or helping with the administration. Whenever the house travels to a distant province the formidable logistics of moving people, baggage and pharmaceuticals would be impossible without the unstinted help of these dedicated angels - and angels they are, exhibiting genuine concern, compassion and caring for any sick person who, as they did, seeks help at the Casa de Dom Inacio.

Space does not permit an explanation of the personal stories of all staff but here are some of them:

The medical practice of Dr. Ronei Pappen MD is situated at Rua Santo Antonio, 653. Porto Alegre. On the 22nd of August 1995, Dr Pappen was involved in a horrific car smash. Without warning, the engine seized and the car catapulted end over end.

Hurled through the windscreen, he suffered massive injuries; his skull was smashed inwards above and behind the right ear. The crushed skull compressed his optical canal and his right eye was hanging out of the socket and peered downwards. He was left totally blind. In addition he had extensive internal injuries and a great deal of skin and flesh were ripped from his legs and back.

Fortunately he knew of Joao and when he regained consciousness in hospital he asked a friend to phone Abadiania. Joao-in-entity advised him not to travel until he had partially recovered as the decompression of a plane trip would cause irreparable damage. He was advised to wait until he was strong enough to travel by car. In the meantime his wounds were stitched and repaired but he was still blind. His colleges said he would never see again.

It was October 12 before Ronei was able to travel by road to Abadiania where the entities performed a number of invisible operations on him. The damage was extensive but over time he regained full eyesight and good health. He now applies his understanding and beliefs of spirit assistance to his own medical practice and dedicates as much time as he can spare to assisting Joao in the house.

Most women of sixty two are retired and touching up their suntan on the beach. But there is one lady of Vitoria, Espirito Santo, who spends her time helping those who are sick. Every second Tuesday around 7 pm you will find her loading up a bus in a back street of Vitoria, 1250 kilometres from Abadiania. Her passengers are not holiday makers they are all sick, suffering with cancer, arthritis, leukaemia, prostrate cancer and many other illnesses, most of them beyond the help of modern medicine.

Dona (Lora) Leuzenita das Neves Nunes delivers her precious cargo over inadequate roads from the coastal city of Vitoria to the mountain village of Abadiania every fortnight to the healing centre of Casa de Dom Inacio, where they undergo treatment by Joao Teixiera de Faria and his Entities.

The gruelling bus ride takes twenty four hours each way and Dona Lora, as she is affectionately known, tends to the needs of her passengers all the way, sometimes without sleep herself. Dona Lora says the pleasure she gets from delivering a bus load of sick to the house and returning with a bus full of happy people on their way to recovery, makes it all worthwhile.

Four years ago there was no way to get to Abadiania when Dona Lora sought desparate help for herself and her ill son. She endured the regular bus service to Brasilia and had to sleep on a bench in the bus terminal until the next morning to catch a local bus to Abadiania. After treatment there was no return service to Brasilia until the next morning so she had to remain overnight. The trip was exhausting, even for a well person but due to her poor state of health it was a nightmare. She and her son needed further treatment so she endured the gruelling trip twice more. On her last trip she was called by the Entity and asked if she could arrange buses for other sick people from Vitoria. When she recovered she looked at the feasibility of hiring a special bus for the direct trip. At first it was not well known and she often had to put money in herself to make ends meet.

These days it is different; Dona Lora is well known at the house and is herself a respected medium who applies any spare time she has to sit 'in current'. She understands the procedures of the centre and ensures that every one of her patients follows the after-healing requirements to ensure their speedy recovery. By word of mouth her bus trips to the healer gained in popularity until now she is well known, sometimes running two buses at a time.

The trip is a tiresome one for even a young healthy person but Dona Lora never complains. To her it has become a way of life. "If I don't do it," she says, "who would help these people get better? I know how I felt when I was sick and some of the people I take to the centre are too ill to survive the regular bus service."

It is not just the organisation of the buses that makes Dona Lora a modern day saint. She also organises a place for the patients to stay overnight, arranges for treatment from the healer and ensures the comfort of each and every patient for the whole trip. Sometimes she even picks them up from their home in her own car to bring them to the bus.

Riding the highways in her 43 seat bus, she can be seen standing in the driver's cabin like a seafaring captain at the helm of his ship. After four years of carrying the ill and crippled to Abadiania there is now a long list of people who owe their new lease of life to this dedicated woman, and the entities of the House of Dom Inacio.

Dona Lora is just one of many tour operators who organize buses to Abadiania from all over Brazil. Beatrix Macedo from Ivoti and Helena of Sta. Maria operate buses every week from Rio Grande do Sul and cover over 6000 klm on their round journey. Others travel from Salvador in the north, Sao Paolo and Rio de Janiero in the south and Matto Grotto do Sul in the southwest. These would be amazing distances on western super highways but on the less than adequate roads of Brazil, they are truly remarkable - and so are the people who travel them.

Registered in the house files is a testimony from a Civil Engineer: *"I came to the House of Dom Inacio to obtain a cure for my daughter who was a classical ballerina. Her legs suddenly began to fail her until she could hardly walk, let alone dance. Allopathic medicines had no effect and she was diagnosed as having tendinitis caused by the dancing, but no examination could prove this. She was a physically healthy girl except for the intense pain in her legs which was so bad she could not walk. When we entered her into the Sara Kubistcheck medical clinic, she had to be carried in on a stretcher. All tests proved normal and inconclusive.*

When we heard about the house we came, and through a period of treatments, she was cured and is now fine. As a form of gratitude for what the entities did for my daughter I come here every Thursday to assist those in need. My daughter and my wife also dedicate time to the house".

On two days each week this engineer runs the administration office of the house, filing the testimonies and the hundreds of letters of gratitude, handling the correspondence as well as assisting in the day to day running of the house when Joao is in entity.

One of the longest serving volunteers is Sebastion da Silver Lima, of Rua Twelve, Quadra 16, Anapolis.

Sebastion was considering entering the priesthood when he first met Joao who invited him to accompany him on an international trip. They have been trusting friends ever since. Theo, as he is affectionately called, has assisted Joao for over twenty six years and says: "Every time I see a smile, a renewed life, I know my work is worthwhile." His main function is as general co-ordinator cum public relations officer. Directing people to receive their treatment, conducting the morning information speeches, organising those who are there for first or second treatments and assisting in the selection of the entity to operate. The importance of this function is to group together like operations so that each entity can operate as quickly and efficiently on as many people as possible.

Theo himself is a powerful medium, although his modesty will not admit it too freely. He, like so many of the helpers, are able to communicate with Joao-in-entity by what is technically known as ESP. Often, whilst speaking to someone, his eyes will stare upwards and he will break away saying only that Entity is 'calling' him. One only has to visit the centre for a few days to experience the remarkable energy of the place. In such an environment this form of inter-communication is not surprising.

Patricia Melo has been a medium of the house for 11 years and is one of only a few English speaking guides who help overseas visitors with the in-house procedures. She can be seen ensuring the smooth flow of foreigners ensuring they get their treatments and understand their follow-up procedures.

An important segment of the house operations is the *current*, the 'power generator' of mediums who sit in meditation and tap into a higher source of energy for Joao-in-entity to utilise in the miraculous cures. There are a hundred or more who, at various times, devote themselves to this important work. Most of these special people came to be cured of their own life-threatening illnesses by the entities and in gratitude now devote their time to the house. One such person was Dona Ilva Ramalho de Menezes.

Dona Ilva was one of the social elite in Brazil, coffee was her husband's business and in their day they lived the high life that money and position provided. But fortunes can be lost quicker than they can be made in Brazil and the Menzies lost most of their wealth, soon after Dona Ilva lost her husband too. She became very ill and sought treatment by her medical doctor. Her condition worsened and the powerful prescription drugs caused her to lose all her beautiful hair. In desperation she sought the help of Joao who, through a number of treatments, cured her illness. Her hair has grown and with it a new set of values. Dona Ilva, now 84 years young, travels the long 1200 klm road to Abadiania by bus every fortnight to sit in current. She is a highly valued member of the house and one of Joao's most powerful and trusted mediums.

One of the most remarkable stories of the house staff is that of Dr. Roger Queiroz who is by profession a Psychologist. Roger, like so many of us, treated life as if there would be no tomorrow living the "good" life without a single notion that there were lessons to be learned on this earthly path.

He had bought his mother to the House of Dom Inacio a few times, the first occasion was sixteen years ago. He remembers his mother saying that the cure required a number of visits and when she said the strange feelings she had inside were a part of the cure by the guides, he just smiled and patted her hand. In his heart he scoffed at this "weird treatment" and viewed the whole thing as ridiculous. He always found it curious though that the people of the house always treated him with such genuine love and affection.

At age 49 his heart was so diseased he would die within a few months if he did not have a major operation. Although he knew about Joao's work he steadfastly refused to accept it and arranged to have a medical operation in Sao Paulo by his doctor colleagues. On the last day he bought his mother to see Joao the Entity "saw" his problem and knew of his intention. Joao-in-Entity took him by the hand and said: "Please do not proceed with the operation. I will cure you." Dr. Roger thanked him kindly but refused the offer.

He arrived in Sao Paulo at 7 am by bus from Brasilia, a gruelling thirty two hour ride. As he stepped down from the bus an old man with grey white hair appeared and spoke to him. "Do you really want to go through with this operation?"

Roger, a bit surprised, replied, "How do you know about my operation?"

The man continued as if he had not heard his remark: "Be sure you know what you are doing my friend."

Roger was now a little offended at this interference and replied somewhat sarcastically: "You seem to know everything, so tell me where the hospital is". He pointed down the road and as Roger turned to look in that direction, the man disappeared.

Roger was booked in at 0900 and scheduled for operation at 1300 hours. As he lay in his bed around 11 o'clock he felt the presence of someone. In defiance he said aloud: "Alright, if you are so concerned, go ahead and heal me!" To his surprise a voice replied: "If you are not operated on immediately you will die". Within minutes Roger suffered a massive cardiac arrest and slipped into unconsciousness. He was rushed to surgery but due to the poor condition of his heart, the operation was not successful. Doctors worked frantically to save him but without success and, after two days in coma, he died.

His wife, Margalie, was still at home in Brazilia. She phoned the hospital just as he passed over. Catapulted into action by the shock of losing her man. She quickly phoned a friend she thought might have Joao's number. At this time the doctors began removing the tubes and resuscitation equipment from his body. The friend looked up the number in her directory, passed it to Margalie who then phoned the house in Abadiania, every minute lost lessened the possibility of Roger's revival.

The phone at the house is in the coffee shop some fifty metres from where Joao works. The girl who took the call ran to Joao-in-entity and told him of the death. Instantly, bearing in mind that there is no time and no space in the spirit plane, the entity restarted the life force of the body now entering the morgue on a trolley. *Roger had been dead for more than thirty minutes!* That he revived was a miracle, that he recovered without any brain damage was astonishing to the doctors who witnessed the event. Roger remembers only that he felt a hand on his shoulder as he came back to life, but there was no one near him at the time.

Roger is now a dedicated volunteer of the house. Every week he stands before the crowds of patients and tells them his story, imploring them to take a good look at their lifestyles, to re-evaluate their beliefs and their attitudes towards their families and friends, and to live in the spirit of charity, caring, consideration and, above all, integrity.

*Author's Note*

On the day I took this story from Dr. Roger he called me from 'current' at around 1415 hours. His uncle was in a hospital in Rio de Janeiro suffering from Hepatitis A, B and C. His liver was so enlarged it was only working spasmodically. The doctors did not expect him to live. A request from Roger's wife to Joao-in-entity for help bought a reply: "Phone your uncle in twenty minutes". Margalie later phoned the hospital and her uncle came on the phone. "I am wonderful", he said. "I can't remember when I felt this good". In that twenty minutes the Entity had treated him in hospital, removed his disease and revitalised his life force.

One of the tireless "angels" of the house is a petite lady with long blond hair. Leonora is the attending nurse in the recovery room. Her gentle compassion and high mediumship qualities make her an ideal "filia da casa" – a child of the house. Leonora volutneers her time, earning a living by providing a guest house for visitors to Abadiania.

Elza has worked voluntarily in the house for the past four years. She prepares the instruments for operation, directs the current room, co-ordinates the function of interviews between patients and the entities and conducts the morning lectures of the house. Her contribution as a co-ordinator of the daily activities is invaluable.

Renate Hock Appel, who lives in Ivoti, first came to the house for a cure for her chronic Rheumatism. That was six years ago. She has volunteered her services to the house ever since. Kind, sweet and compassionate, her ever helpful nature is a welcome introduction to the house for many sick and disoriented people who seek her direction. Renate also assists in the running of the intensive operations room and conducts the pre-operation talks when required.

Orvalino da Costa has worked in the house ever since Joao cured him of severe haemorrhoids and a chronic eye problem, one and a half years ago. Orvalino directs the assembly of patients queuing to be interviewed by the entities. He helps carry the operated patients to the recovery room and assists in the organisation of the physical surgery. Orvalino, who remembers well the need for direction when he first came to the house, is always ready to direct a new patient with kindness and sympathy.

Geraldo Adao Porrecuppi of Contagem M.G., has helped out in the house for the past four years, ever since Joao cured his 20 year old son from a serious spinal injury suffered when his car plunged over a cliff. Geraldo directs the main current room and assists in the conduct of the physical surgery.

Jose Roberto Batista Brum, a tall handsome professor of technical studies at Escola Tecnica Federal de Goias, first came to the house in a dreadful state. He was living in Rio de Janiero at the time and suffered from severe leg pains which almost crippled him. He developed sores all over his body and he was convinced that he had AIDS. The thought terrified him and the more he dwelled on it the worse the sores became. Medical attempts to alleviate his condition bought no relief. A workmate, who often went to Abadiania, took a photo and bought back herbs for him. Upon seeing the photo the Entity requested Roberto come personally to the house and as the herbs began to have a beneficial effect, Robert felt compelled to oblige.

A few weeks later Roberto stood before the Entity: "My son", he said, "the reason you are sick is because you are a powerful medium and you have suppressed it. The suppressed energy is causing your illness. You must expend it or you will not get well". Roberto moved his family from Rio four years ago and has worked at the house ever since, arranging his lectures to fit around his voluntary duties. His powerful medium qualities and organizational skills are a welcome input at Abadiania.

These days the smooth introduction of English/Spanish speaking foreigners to the entities for healing would be sadly lacking if it were not for the wonderfully selfless work of Martin. A handsome charming and humble man who can be seen leading people to Joao-in-entity, ensuring they understand the procedures and answering their infinite questions. Martin owes the life of his mother and his beautiful wife to the work of the entities, in gratitude he serves as guide and interpreter.

Space does not permit a listing of all the children of the house; those wonderful young nurses who tenderly care for the patients in the post operations room, the dispensers of herbs who work feverishly to issue upwards of 5000 bottles of herbs a day often without a break in a long ten hour shift, the mediums who sit in meditation for four hours or more each session, the cooks who prepare up to 3000 plates of soup per day, the assistants who help during the physical surgery and organise the long line of patients, the video personnel, the cleaners, the gardeners and importantly, the staff of directors who take the ultimate responsibility for the running of the House of Dom Inacio.

Many of the personnel mentioned above have since returned to their pre-illness lives. New staff and volunteers come and go, all give their time freely and in gratitude.

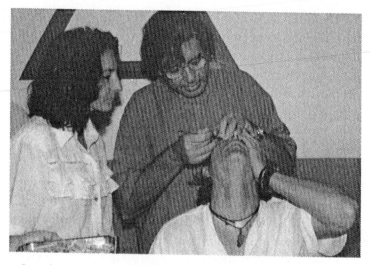

Joao-in-entity performs an eye operation without anaesthetic.

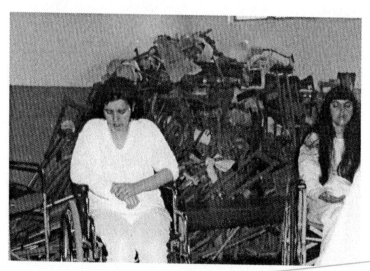

Handicapped sit in meditation. Behind a mountain of discarded
wheelchairs, braces and crutches.

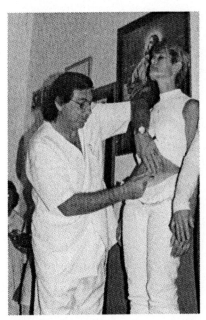

Joao-in-entity operates for a tumour.

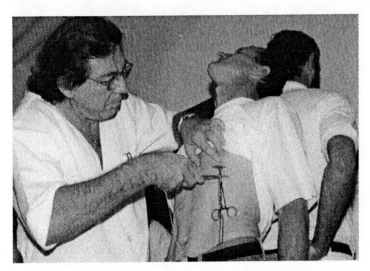

Joao performs heart surgery without anaesthetic or pain.

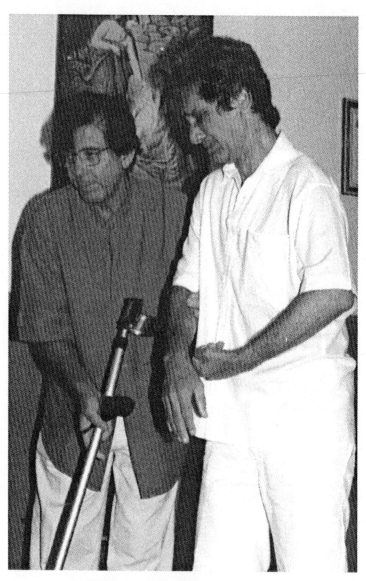

Joao encourages a stroke victim to walk.

Four of Joao's guides.
Clockwise from top left:
Dom Inacio
Dr. Almeida
Dr. Menezes
Dr. Cruz

Every day up to 3,000 people queue to see the 'Entity'.

## Chapter 7

# Rich, Poor And Famous

*Sickness is the great leveller of all mankind. There is an equality amongst all sick, no matter their status in life.*
The Author

Of the multitudes who come to Joao for help the largest percentage are poor or with little material wealth. There are, of course, many who are of high position within government or society, and some are rich beyond the average person's comprehension - all are equal in his eyes. Each one is just a soul with a sick body or a sick mind reaching out for relief from their physical pain. Although he treats hundreds of thousands each year, it is only when someone of social prominence and wealth, who has access to the most modern and expensive medical expertise science can offer, is successfully treated that we can compare the extent of his extraordinary capabilities.

Prominent and well known people from all over the world have sought his help when modern medicine has given them up. Those who have been successfully treated by Joao and the entities include actress Shirley Maclean and others who came in secret. Congressmen and congresswomen, politicians, lawyers, rabbis, priests, nuns, American and Russian government officials, doctors, scientists, singers, entertainers, millionaires, entrepreneurs, industrialists and VIPs; the whole broad spectrum of humanity. Perhaps the most reported case was that of actress Shirley Maclean who is a very spiritually aware person and a living example that spirituality, humility and concern for your fellow man are not restricted to the underprivileged. That these virtues can be comfortable companions on the journey of life, regardless of one's status. Her story is best told by the media headlines following her trip to Abadiania:

*MANCHETE EXCLUSIVE. 2 MARCH 1991*
by Fernando Pinto..

**Medium operates on Shiley MacLaine.**

*BRASILIA, Yesterday. The American singer actress, Ms Shirley Maclean underwent a 'spiritual operation' to extract a cancer from her abdomen. She arrived in Brazilia on Thursday feeling great pain.*

*Ms. Maclean arrived in Abadiania (GO), some 120 km. from Brazilia, suffering from great pain. After the 'spiritual operation' effected by the medium, Joao Teixeira de Faria ( known also as Joao de Deus and Joao the Healer), the actress, according to eye witnesses, showed deep emotion at what had been done and declared that she no longer felt pain.*

*The operation was performed on her by the entity, Dr. Augusto de Almeida, incorporated by Joao de Deus during an operation lasting nearly two hours. During the spiritual operation the actress lay on a table covered with a white sheet.*

*The operation was done entirely with the hands, with which the medium extracted the tumour from the actress' body. No knives or other instruments were used. The operation greatly moved all present at the spiritual session held in the room called The House of Blessing, where Joao de Deus works.*

*The actress left Abadiania by car and went straight to Brasilia. She stayed at the Hotel Eron, one of the five star hotels in that city. The reservation had been confirmed and cancelled several times. This strategy, planned to avoid the press, had also been used by the pilot of the plane which crossed the skies of the western centre without passengers.*

*Ms Maclean's visit to the Valley of Sunrise - locally and internationally know for its mysticism - was confirmed today.*

Five days later, on 7th March 1991, the story was confirmed by reporter Monica Prado in the newspaper O GLOBO:

### Medium confirms operation on MacLaine

*The actress's visit to Abadiania has been documented. Abadiania's medium Joao Teixeira who, last Friday gave a spiritual healing to the American actress Ms. Shirley Maclean, both denied and confirmed some facts: contrary to what the actress said during her hurried interview in Rio de Janeiro to the O GLOBO reporter who spread the news of Ms Maclean's visit to Abadiania, she did not suffer from a tumour of the brain. The actress had in fact a cancer of the stomach. The medium states that, through a spiritual operation, the tumour was eliminated.*

*'She was here and told only me what she had. For ethical reasons, I am not permitted to reveal further details. Neither can I say much, being an 'unconscious medium' I don't know what my entity did.'*

*Even though the actress may not wish to confirm it, she left a record of her illness and its cure to the people responsible for the (work in) the House of Blessing where the medium Joao acts. In her book 'Going Within: a Guide for Inner Transformation', Shirley reveals that she undertook a series of unsuccessful operations in the Philippines.*

*When some people who were at the house asked the actress why she sought Joao Teixeira, she explained that she had a dream in which it was revealed that the medium was the only one who could heal her. After the session in the operating room, Shirley, with her hand on her breast said with emotion:*

*'I am cured. I no longer feel pain!'*

*The co-ordinator of the spiritual work in the house, Sebastion Lima, added:*

*'Shirley was deeply stirred and smiling. When she left the room of spiritual cure, she skipped a bit and said: "Now I can dance again!"*

*She took home a bottle of water and was advised to avoid eating chillies, pork, bananas, eggs and alcohol.' he said.*

*'She hugged me several times to show that she recognised in the operation a serious spiritual work, 'said Joao Teixeira. He added that he considered her an extremely*

*"spirtualized" person and was a little surprised at the mysterious atmosphere she created around her coming to Abadiania. 'All people are special to me. She did not receive any different treatment because she is a famous actress.'*

*The actress's passage and the spiritual cure were documented by one of the six members of the group that accompanied her, among whom was the ex-Deputy Ruth Escobar.*

*The treatment given to the actress, according to Joao Teixeira, was effected solely by energy of the hands without the use of instruments. The spiritual operation done with the hands is also known as 'operation without surgery' or 'invisible'.*

*The American ex-Deputy Bella Abzug who had accompanied Ms. Maclean, was operated with surgical instruments. The operation proved to be easy and she was given medicines from the pharmacy of the house. Just like the 'invisible operation' of Shirley's, Bella's operation was documented on video, taped by Ruth Escobar."*

MANCHETE MAGAZINE, the equivalent of America's LIFE MAGAZINE, ran a four page article on the visit in the 16th of March 1991 issue - story by Fernando Pinto:

***Joao De Deus - A medium in the path of Shirley MacLaine.***

*Shirley Maclean smiled on arrival then, deeply moved, she entered Joao de Deus' room.*

*She came from the back, her face almost hidden. There were two big cars; a black Landau in which she travelled and a red car with a woman and a man, believed to be lawyers. They did not want to leave the cars. First they wanted to know if the MANCHETE reporters were here. If they were present they would leave without coming out of the cars as Ms. Maclean did not wish to be photographed.*

*By that time it was already nearly 4.30 in the afternoon and work was almost finished. Mario Reis said. 'Joao, being busy, told me to take care of Ms. Shirley and her friends, one of whom I learned was Deputy Ruth Escobar, and it was Ruth who asked me to take away all the cameras from the house, even those belonging to the house photographer. I spoke again with Joao and he told me to oblige. Only then did Ms. Maclean come in, smiling at me in such a lovely way, just as she did in her pictures.*

*There she watched Joao performing some operations and even helped, carrying the tray with instruments. Only after that did she enter the spiritual operations room. I waited outside, when Ms. Shirley came back I noticed she looked somewhat different.'*

*There are three things Tiao (the house co-ordinator, Mr Sebastion Lima) will not forget about Shirley Maclean's visit to Abadiania on that historical March 1st, 1991: the fact that she tried to speak to him in Spanish, the feminine perfume and the unforgettable leave they took of each other: 'Before entering the Landau she hugged me and said some words I didn't understand. When I looked at her she was crying, deeply moved, I cried too.'*

*Ms. Maclean may have cried when she departed but did not move a muscle during the 'operation on her abdomen'. This testimony was given by physician Sonia Maria Lira, aged 49, graduate from the Faculty of Medicine of Valencia. She is one of the few persons who admits having been at the actress's side when she submitted to the spiritual lancet of Dr. Jose Augusto, incorporated by the medium from Goias, Joao Teixeira, aged 45, better known as Joao de Abadiania or Joao de Deus."*

One could naturally be tempted to think that such a miraculous healing gift should be bestowed upon the most educated, intelligent or influential of our species. One might also be forgiven in assuming that such a man would be honoured, revered and rewarded with wealth and prestige. In proportion to the value of returning health and life, one would at least expect respect from one's fellow man, especially in an age where we pride ourselves for our highly developed sense of justice and our lavish appreciation of far lesser achievements.

Quite the opposite is the truth of the life of this dedicated and extraordinarily gifted man. His fellow man, full of jealousy, suspicion and false ego, bestowed upon him their relentless venom. Fortunately for the multitudes he has helped, the spirits chose well; *a man, not of cultivated society or extreme intellect, but one of exceptional courage, perseverance and, above all, an unswerving dedication to his life's mission, who makes no preferential judgement of colour, class, wealth, religion or position. This is a man worthy of his common title - John of God.*

## Chapter 8

# Understanding Spiritualism

*Spititualism : The belief that the disembodied spirits of the dead, surviving
in another world, can communicate with the living in this world, especially
through mediums.*
Oxford English Dictionary.

I lay on a simple table in a small corrugated iron shack
stripped to the waist. The young man standing over me quietly
and humbly whispered his prayers, hands turned upwards, eyes
closed. Attunement completed, Ambrioso pointed two fingers
together toward my abdomen and, on contact with the skin,
pulled them apart, opening my flesh like a warm knife through
butter.

I was awake and watched calmly as the incision spread
open. There was no pain and virtually no blood. I was not
medically anaesthetised. I was not hypnotised. I suffered no
trauma and there was no visible sterilisation. Ambrosio closed
the incision with a simple wipe of his palm leaving a barely
discernible thin pink scar which would disappear within two
days. I had been operated on by spirit surgery.

I was to experience nine more operations during the next
three days. I was free to take any photograph I wished and I
could subject him to any examination. The operations had little
if any ill effect on me. After each session I dressed and walked
the two kilometres back to my hotel with no discomfort or pain.

Ambrosio is a Philippino healer medium who calls on spirit to
supply energy to perform surgery or healing. A devout believer

in God and the Holy Spirit but, unlike Joao, he does not incorporate a spirit and retains awareness of his actions throughout all surgery and healing. He calls on spirit by prayer to supply the energy through his body like a receiver/transmitter. These energies are real and powerful but little known in our physical world.

In the case of paralysis like Raul, the man in the wheelchair (Chapter 1), Joao-in-entity was able to look inside the body, see the pressures on nerve structures, see deficiencies in nerve plexuses that needed replenishing, and could identify forces of the body that control the locomotory system. He could see incoordination between the autonomic nervous systems of the body and provide the curative energy necessary to "kick start" his nervous system.

### Spirit Energies.

Spiritism and spirit energies can be likened to magnetism, electricity or gravity. The results of their existence are observable but they cannot be seen in themselves. Less than two hundred years ago experimentation in unseen forces such as electricity was considered black magic and people who dabbled in them were proclaimed weird and often put to death. Today some of these unseen forces are accepted, and some are still considered as 'paranormal'.

Dr john Ott, a respected American scientist who has studied light, colour and energy for over thirty years states that we utilize less than 1% of the known electromagnetic spectrum of energies.

### Spiritism.

What then is Spiritism? Is it a miraculous occurrence, to be feared, revered and left to the questionable ritualisms of religion? Allan Kardic, the 19th century author, medium and spiritist insists that spiritism should not be classified as miraculous but as a universal law. *"Like magnetism, it reveals a law - the law known, the marvellous disappears, and the phenomena re-enters the natural state of things. It is no more miraculous than all the other phenomena due to invisible agents ( electricity, radiation, micro waves etc.) because these (spirit) beings, who people space, are one of the powers of nature. They are a natural phenomena."*

There are two main issues involved in the understanding of spirit healing. Both require the acceptance of the existence of a vast spirit world which works in harmony and synchronisation with our physical world. They are, firstly, that our spirit lives on after death and, secondly, that there exist many energies available to spirit of which we have little or no

"Both matter and spirit are energy forces. They are simply of different frequencies. They are not as far apart as might be thought. The spirit loses the shell of the body, as a caterpillar loses its cocoon. But the personality remains conscious and aware."
*Unknown medium.*

knowledge. Both of these are observable in the daily workings of Joao. His seemingly amazing cures and operations can only be classified as miracles by those who refuse to accept the reality of spirit assistance.

That the spirit lives on after death is supported by so many documented cases it is a slight on our western society not to be taught of its existence from birth. If we were, perhaps humanity would live in closer harmony in the knowledge that all indiscretions must be accounted for eventually, and that there is a very real purpose for our existence in this life beyond the accumulation of material wealth.

Western society has lost connection with its spirit origins. In countries like India, Brazil and China the existence of a spirit world, living and working around us in our daily lives, is totally acceptable. Most people in these countries live their lives within this "knowing", regulating their daily actions in accordance with the universal laws of love, honesty, morality, humility, charity and consideration knowing that their actions will be the basis on which they are either elevated or lowered at the conclusion of their current life. Western society in the 90's spasmodically reacts, in a knee jerk reaction, with every new book or media focus in a new age fanaticism which lasts only as long as the memory of the exposure.

There are so many respected studies of life after death that is difficult to select but a few to illustrate the point. Interviews by author researcher Kenneth Ring of hundreds of out-of-body-death (OBD) experiences resulted in striking similarities. Each person became aware of the death of their body and their subsequent entry into an indescribable light of love and joy, an ecstatic encounter with loving beings of light and often a reunion with departed loved ones. All described a flash review of their lives and how, even the smallest indiscretion caused them a blush of regret.

> "I have spoken with many in the spirit world who, prior to their passing, did not believe in an after life, believing rather that being dead means no more life - no more anything. Each time I hear them express their surprise and delight upon discovering survival after death." Rosemary Altea, *The Eagle and the Rose.*

So why have not the spirits themselves talked to us to reveal their existence? They have, and they continue to do so. Joao Teixeira de Faria almost daily permits his body to be used as a vessel to convey messages from the spirit plane. From simple demands to live a cleaner life to profound insights of knowledge only available from the source. These messages are delivered at random during surgery and healings and are video recorded every day. There are literally thousands of hours of recordings freely available to the public at a nominal cost.

### The Edgar Casey Readings.

Joao is not the only medium to convey messages from spirits. Another well known and carefully recorded medium was America's Edgar Casey who recorded no less than fourteen thousand "readings"(messages) dealing with healing, nutrition, health, religion, reincarnation and the origins of man. During self induced sleep he received the information directly from the spirits themselves. On the origins of man and reincarnation of the soul there was no greater insight. An interpretation by his son, Hugh Lynn Casey, provides an authoritative understanding of man's materialisation from spirit form and how man lost his connection to this original form because of selfishness and self indulgence. The following explanation is a remarkable insight into the creation of man and his current distance from his spirit origins.

*"Some of the original spiritual creations or souls who had taken on materiality for their own diversion had in a sense become trapped in it. By misusing their creative powers in self-indulgence, they became subject to the laws of cause and effect which include the laws of karma and reincarnation. These "Sons of Belial", as they were called in the readings, continued their selfish exploitation of the earth and its life forms until they lost sight of their true spiritual nature. This may have been the real fall of man. A soul that has so separated itself from its maker by selfishness that, even after death it cannot comprehend its own nature but is drawn back into what it has created, is indeed in hell. However some of these souls realised their predicament and attempted to create a vehicle (man) through which it would be possible for souls to regain a comprehension of their Creator. I believe these efforts culminated in Christ who voluntarily took human form to show man the path home."*

### *Allan Kardec, the Father of Spiritism.*

Allan Kardec, too, received his information directly from spirit. In his book *The Book on Mediums* he gives a remarkable description of death and the separation of the dead into three parts: the *body* shell, the *spirit* or soul and the *perispirit*: *"The spirit incarnated in the body constitutes the soul; when it leaves the body at death, it does not leave it entirely stripped of an envelope. All (spirits) tell us they preserve the human form and, in fact, when they appear to us it is in the human form in which we have known them. At the moment they leave this life they are in a troubled state, everything around them is confused; they see their body, whole or mutilated, according to the kind of death: on the other hand, they see themselves and feel that they are living. When this first troubled moment dissipates the body becomes for them like an old garment which they have stripped off and no longer regret; they feel lighter as if disencumbered of a burden. They no longer feel pain and are perfectly happy in the power of elevating themselves, traversing space as they have a thousand times in their dreams while living. In the meantime they realise they have a form"* (in spite of the absence of the body).

*"There are in man three things: first the soul or spirit, an intelligent principle in which resides the moral sense; second, the body, gross material envelope with which it is clothed; third, the perispirit, semi-material, fluid envelope serving as a link between the soul and the body.*

> "...the physical body is only the current vehicle of our spirit as it lives and learns in the earth dimension." Robert Monroe, *Ultimate Journey.*

*Death is the destruction or disintegration of the grosser envelope - that which the soul abandons; the other (perispirit) is disengaged and follows the soul which thus finds itself always in possession of an envelope, fluid, ethereal, vaporous, invisible to us in its normal state. This second envelope of the soul is the intermediary of all sensations perceived by the spirit which it transmits to the exterior and acts upon the organs. It is the conductor, the electric thread which serves for the reception and transmission of thought; that mysterious unseizable agent, denominated nervous fluid of which too little is thought in physiological and pathological phenomena. Medicine, considering only the material (physical) element, is deprived of an incessant cause of action. Knowledge of the perispirit is the key to a crowd of (medical) problems hitherto inexplicable."*

More recently, in an extensive study of the amazing Brazilian healer Ze Arigo by industrialist, pharmaceutical manufacturer and respected psychiatrist Luis Rodrigues, who points to Arigo's ability to perform apparently miraculous surgery by spirit incorporation, as does Joao. The spirit who used his body was that of Dr. Adolph Fritz, a gifted and forthright German surgeon who died prematurely during World War I. Rodrigues statement, whilst intended for Arigo, applies equally to the incorporations of Joao: *"This close collaboration between (the medium) and his discarnate friends (spirit entities) cannot be understood unless these basic hard facts of life are taken into account:*

1. That man is an incarnate soul.

2. This soul was not created at the time of birth.

3. It has lived many lives on earth and that others will consequently follow.

4. That contact between incarnate and discarnate persons has been taking place since man appeared on earth for the first time.

5. The psychic faculty known as mediumship is the method devised by nature to establish this necessary and enlightening contact.

6. That primitive peoples all over the world are well acquainted with these simple facts of life.

*What I have learned is that it behoves us to improve this contact. Separating it from the superstitions involved in religious creeds, doctrines or dogmas from rites and rituals. Likewise, do not waste time with obdurate scepticism that retards progress by postulating pseudo-scientific explanations that explain nothing."*

Rodrigues displays a refreshing directness in this statement urging us not to waste time looking for elusive alternate explanations for the extraordinary healing and surgical methods of gifted mediums such as Arigo and Joao. He has not, however, explored the link between healing and the role played by spirit awareness, and the subsequent need to live a life based on a core set of universal principles; truth, honesty, integrity, charity and compassion.

The entities, whilst incorporated in Joao, daily instruct us on the existence of the spirit world; urging us to live a better life and warning us that, under the Laws of Cause and Effect, criminal or deceitful indiscretions must eventually be paid for by karmic debt. This debt can be unexplainable illness or misfortunes, both in this life and subsequent lives.

Ultimately, we need to understand that the real purpose of our current and subsequent lives is to elevate our soul to a point of perfection. We have been given only one facility with which to control the direction of our lives; *our free will.* With this we must make a multitude of small decisions each day, good or bad, right or wrong, according to the universal laws of charity, honesty, tolerance and a love of your fellow man as you love yourself.

### Spirits, Good or Bad?

Are there bad spirits? Most decidedly. Kardec states that, *"as there are bad and good people, so there are bad and good spirits."* A very bad person becomes a very bad spirit in the hereafter just as a saintly person becomes a good spirit. Spirits can be frivolous, vengeful, suffering, lonely or just plain bad but elevated spirits are none of these, they believe in good and, depending on their particular state of elevation, will work with us to do good and help us elevate too. And, of course, just as there are techniques to gain assistance from good spirits, there are techniques called rituals, or black magic, for gaining the assistance of the bad. In many societies and countries this is readily recognised.

In Brazil the existence of spirit, good and bad, is recognised by the larger proportion of the population. Brazil's spiritual beliefs can be divided into three basic types; the predominating Catholicism, Quimbanda (black magic) and the softer more Christian style of Umbanda. The later two grew out of the early days of harsh Brazilian slavery. Both embrace a belief in spirit possession and magical rites. Brought from Africa by black African slaves, they were used vengefully against their cruel masters. Quimbanda black magic is still used to this day and, like Christian book shops in the western world, there are many retail stores throughout Brazil where ritual paraphernalia can be purchased. It is not uncommon to encounter people who have had a spell placed on them by this means. At Abadiania Joao encounters these situations frequently.

One sad case was a beautiful young lady who was to be married in six weeks when she came to Joao for help. Her fiancee's previous girlfriend had paid to have a Macumba spell placed on her. Her luxurious long black hair fell out in handfuls. The entity in Joao immediately recognised the possession and expelled it. The couple were happily married six weeks later with a healthy, albeit short haired, bride.

The short-sightedness of modern psychiatry fails to recognise that many functional neurosis and psychoses are the result of possessions - attachments of disenchanted spirit into a receptive vessel; a depressed, lonely, weak or ill person. (See chapter 6 - Causes of Illness).

### Poltergeists.

Finally, it is necessary to touch on the existence of Poltergeists. Contrary to popular belief Poltergeists do exist, thankfully they are rare for they can create havoc when they vent their frivolity or anger. A Poltergeist is simply a spirit of lower level which, for a variety of reasons, decides to make its presence known, in a physical manner. It may have an attachment to a certain place, perhaps where it used to live or where a loved one still resides. It may be held there because it was miserly and won't let go of material possessions or it could be angry about events that happened there, but for whatever reason they can be troublesome. Exorcism in the religious manner rarely succeeds. Capricious spirits can find it amusing and intensify the activity for their own amusement. Such was the case of the phenomena at the Fazenda Mondongo.

In December 1990, Joao was called to disperse a spirit manifestation, which was causing havoc with farm labourers on the isolated farmlet, Fazenda Mondongo, 80 kilometres from Pirenopolis, Goiana. Eight farmhands who were living in the isolated ranch were experiencing horrific physical treatment of nightly beatings and stonings by a spirit entity. Even when the men locked themselves inside the farmhouse the entity materialised logs which it threw around the rooms. Knives were removed from the kitchen cupboard and thrown with amazing accuracy close to the heads of the workers. During the day shovels would begin to dig by themselves, throwing the soil at the workers with intermittent slapping of their faces.

This was a true Poltergeist and any attempt to dispel it proved fruitless, more over, any attempt only increased the activity. The story soon spread and caught the attention of reporter, Marconi Barreto, who photographed and reported it in the national newspaper, *Diario da Manha*. Someone recommended that Joao be consulted. When he arrived at the Fazenda the entity defiantly increased activity. Joao did not attempt to bully it into leaving but encouraged it gently with reassurances that calmed its anger. He used soft candle light instead of electric light and meditated to call on higher level spirit to dispel the lower entity. Finally, after some days, the entity left and has never returned.

Unfortunately there is a great deal of ignorance and scepticism about spirit and, what is called, the supernatural. The understanding that spirits and their energies exist is only limited by our physical comprehension in our ponderous physical world. This invisible being, to which we have given the name of spirit, is none other than the soul of those who have lived corporeally and whom death has stripped of their gross, visible envelope, leaving them only an ethereal envelope, invisible in its normal state.

In dying, they have lost only their body but have retained intelligence which is their essence. That is the key to all the phenomena erroneously reported as *supernatural*.

*The body shell is transitory – The spirit is immortal.*

*Chapter 9*

# The Causes Of Disease

*Our physical bodies exist within a larger "body", a human energy field,
which is the vehicle through which we create our experience of reality,
including health and illness* (it) *is the starting point of all illness.*
Barbara Ann Brennan. "Hands of Light".

To understand the energies and methods of healing and
surgery used by Joao through his entities requires an understanding of universal energies of which we are only able to grasp
the fringe, but one portion of understanding that has developed
in recent years is that of the Human Energy Field. This scientifically acknowledged bioplasmic field of seven coloured layers is
the defence system of the physical body. Most diseases begin
first in these protective layers before the symptoms manifest in
the body. If the fields are distorted, unbalanced and vibrating
badly due to constant disharmony, disease will form and mate-
rialise into the dense physical body. Weaknesses or fissures in
the fields can also allow "attachments" to take hold with a
variety of symptoms from sleeplessness to serious psychosis.
One remarkable case from the video files of the House of Dom
Inacio is that of the woman who cried tears of blood.

## Undesirable Attachments

The young woman had been unwell for a long time. She did
not sleep well; the images disturbed her. They were beyond her
control. She felt tired, weary and sometimes she would loose
control altogether and slip into trace. When she regained con-

sciousness there was always blood streaming from her eyes - she literally cried blood!

This naturally beautiful young lady with long golden ringlets and blue eyes had an attachment: she was possessed by the spirit of her grandmother! The spirit within her was not aggressive but it controlled her. It carried its own experiences and memories and transferred to her host, images of past lives which, in the absence of a logical explanation, she silently believed to be a mental problem. She felt she was going crazy.

When she came to the house, Joao instructed her to sit and meditate with the mediums in the 'current'. The spirit within rebelled and would not allow her to enter the room for two days, but on the third day the woman overcame the grandmother's will and sat in meditation with the mediums. Within a short time a conflict began in which the spirit took control, causing the girl to stand up and, in semi-trance, made her dance in a slow flowing Dance of the Veils. The young lady saw herself as a dancer in an Arabian tent - she was glimpsing a portion of one of her grandmother's past lives. As the dance progressed the Entity could see and talk to the spirit. The spirit was soothed and reassured that the granddaughter would be alright without her help; it should not concern itself with her well-being and should move on to where it belongs. Eventually the spirit was coaxed into departing. The dance slowed, then ceased, leaving the girl with streams of blood from her eyes. She is now healthy, sleeps well and is free of her caring burden.

This remarkably graphic example of possession is a rare phenomenon, but spirit attachment is not! Illness caused by spirit attachment is more common than we realise. Such illness can most often be traced to weakened energy field defences in which undesirable attachments gain access to the body. Depression, prolonged sadness or mourning, excessive emotional stress and drug and alcohol abuse create a comfortable home for low spirit attachments which can leave the host body feeling debilitated, depressed and suffering from many of the maladies of the attached spirit: sore back, lethargy, depression and other symptoms which are impossible for doctors to diagnose.

There is a spreading belief amongst respected psychiatrists throughout the world that a large proportion of mental illness in the western societies is the result of spirit attachments. One who is leading this thought is industrialist and respected psychiatrist, Luis Rodriguez who pulls no punches in his opinion of the extent of spirit possession:

"I have been preoccupied for many years with the failure of psychiatry to identify the aetiology, or origin, of functional neurosis and psychoses which, in more than eighty percent of cases, is nothing else but symptoms and syndromes revealing the flourishing of possession.

Failure to identify these syndromes for what they are has converted hundreds of thousands of individuals in the civilised world who are not sick, into schizophrenics. Mental hospitals are full of them. This happens when electric shock, insulin or chemical drugs are induced in them blocking the natural manifestations of mediumship, destroying the mechanism through which the faculty manifests itself. The same occurs with the wholesale use of tranquillisers.

"Look on an attached spirit as we would bacterium. When we are healthy, our immune system takes care of even deadly bacterium. When our immune is weakened or damaged, then bacteria or viruses enter to create havoc. The same can be said for spirit attachment. If one's energy field is healthy and strong, spirits will not be able to enter. If the field is weakened by illness, drugs, accidents, etc., then an opening is created for the spirit." George Schwimmer, *Contractual Agreement.*

The so-called 'witch doctors' and the spiritists of the reincarnation school all over the world quickly recognise these symptoms for what they really are. As a consequence of this knowledge, mediumship is developed instead of psychosis. The development eradicates the psychoneurotic or psychotic condition. This is the reason why mental diseases do not exist among these people, who may be counted in the millions.

Mental diseases are, therefore, the fruit harvested by over-civilised man due exclusively to a condition of ignorance maintained by an exaggerated sense of sophistication and hallowed cultural superiority!"

Illness due to spirit attachment is a common occurrence and readily accepted by a growing number of western therapists. Dr. Edith Fiore, a California psychologist and author of the trail-blazing book on spirit attachment, *The Unquiet Dead,* states that depressions can often be traced to despondent spirits who do not know that they are dead.

> "A bodily disease, which we look upon as whole and entire within itself, may after all, be but a symptom of some ailment in the spirit part."
> Nathaniel Hawthorne, *The Scarlet Letter (1850).*

She says that in hundreds of cases she has cured patients of alcoholism or depression by releasing the attached spirits suffering from these problems. If, however, the host was an alcoholic when the spirit arrived it is probable they will still be an alcoholic when the spirit leaves. Dr. Fiore claims that the majority of people, perhaps as many as 90 percent, probably suffer from some form of spirit attachment!

The old exorcism rites of the Roman Catholic Church and other religions in which the 'lost' spirit is treated as some sort of demon to be driven out of the host body, is not in keeping with the love teachings of these same religions. Rather these attachments are lost souls, usually family members who are afraid or in need of guidance. As is often observed in Abadiania, Joao coaxes them to let go, seek the light, and exit gently from the earth plane in company with deceased loved ones or accompanying spirits.

In the readings of American Edgar Casey, the famous 'sleeping prophet', there are many references to spirit attachment. He too was careful to point out that individuals were not possessed by demons, the devil, nor evil spirits. Rather they were possessed by the spirits of those who had died and refused to move on to other planes in the afterlife. Such spirits were refereed to as 'earthbound' because their appetites during their physical lives were so strong as to be addictive. The addictive personality, whether it had been for alcohol, drugs, cigarettes, sex, food, money or power is evidently more likely to try to satisfy the cravings after death in any way he/she can, even to the point of attachment to a person who has similar cravings. Hence drug or alcohol abusers, almost without exception, attract lost soul attachments who were drug and alcohol abusers themselves, and still crave the habit. They can be very abusive and cantankerous if force is used to make them leave their comfortable and satisfying environment.

The causes of spirit attachments are varied, rarely due to a single cause. Severe injury, excessive sadness at the loss of a loved one, excesses of life, imbalances in physical or mental co-ordinations, and frequently, amateur experiments in psychic or spiritual studies. Some spiritually or psychically sensitive individuals, without proper guidance and preparation in spiritual experiments, leave themselves open to outside influences by negative discarnates (souls between earth incarnations). Many consider themselves as spiritually advanced without recognising the corresponding responsibility to live up to such standards.

There is hardly a day at the House of Dom Inacio when there is not at least one, if not numerous cases requiring the dispelling of undesirable attachments. In acute cases, they can be seen writhing, shaking, moaning or sobbing uncontrollably in the current line of the cleansing room. It is quite common to see a person writhing like a snake whilst portraying a torpid reptilian stare.

Many wale and sob uncontrollably and others stare out through old and lost eyes that show their disapproval at being disturbed from their comfortable resting place of misery.

Joao treats every soul with dignity and respect. Such spirit releasement works specifically with the soul of the deceased which attaches itself to the consciousness of the living. That soul may need assistance in recognising it is dead, to move on and not remain attached to the earth plane.

### Pressures of Modern Civilisation.

There are, of course, a proliferation of illnesses caused by exposure to our modern lifestyle. We attempt to tolerate pressures with which we were never meant to cope; psychological pressures from work, unhappy or broken marriages and society's demanding expectations. Chemical exposure in our environment, over refined foods containing chemical additives, drugs, smoking and alcohol, all create pressures on our minds and bodies which invariably result in sickness, disability and deformity.

We have become accustomed to taking pills and synthetic "wonder drugs" to alleviate undesirable symptoms, or consulting a medical practitioner who will prescribe more drugs in a silent 'experiment' to correct our problems. If the ailment persists we are ultimately hospitalised. The long waiting time for patients requiring non essential or exploratory surgery is testimony to western society's inability to cope with the burgeoning number of sick.

Not surprisingly, the taking of more and more medications often result in a temporary relief of the symptoms but do nothing to correct the problem in the body and at the source. From the files of the house there is overwhelming evidence that excessive or unnecessary pharmaceuticals can do irreparable damage.

One prominent case is the rancher, Arnilo Valter Matrin of Rio Grande de Sul, who went to his dentist for a simple extraction. His mouth became infected and the dentist injected massive amounts of antibiotics into his gums to suppress the inflamation. He became very ill and totally lost his eyesight, in addition he received powerful drugs for his seriously diseased liver and kidneys and two tumours in his chest. When his condition continued to deteriorate and the doctors gave up, he went to the house as a last desperate hope. Joao and the entities successfully treated his body but could not immediately replace his eyesight; it had been severly damaged by the drugs to a point where it was almost irreparable.

Volter, in gratitude, now dedicates his time to the house. He makes the return journey of 6000km by bus every two weeks to give his services. He can be seen sitting in the current room with his dark glasses and his white cane propped beside him. He is still hopeful of regaining his eyesight but it will take a very long time.

### The Tongue.

Before every healing session in the house, there is one or more talks delivered to the audience waiting in the main hall. The talks cover many subjects including an explanation of spiritism, a reassurance that the house is non sectarian, explanations about the medicinal herbs and water and how people should live and respect their fellow man. This last subject is dealt with in some detail; it is called *"sickness of the tongue"*.

Of all the thousands who come to Abadiania with their various maladies, a large percentage can be traced back to unkind words as the root cause of the illness. Human beings have a remarkable ability to communicate with

> "People ask for criticism, but they only want praise." W. Somerset Maugham, *Of Human Bondage (1915)*.

the spoken word in multiple languages and an infinite range of nuances and suggestive overtones. The power of communication has been the means whereby many of the world's dictators gained control of nations through persuasive oratory. We do not have to look far to find some unhappy examples; Hitler, Stalin and Mussolini all left behind legacies of misery and destruction that the world will long remember. The destruction wreaked by each of us every day with unkind words, snide remarks or all out verbal attacks on our relatives, friends and loved ones is just as destructive as any physical punishment.

Human beings are highly sensitive to the world around them. Their conscious mind protects them from unkind verbal attack with retaliation and reason but the less focused subconscious mind, does not have this ability to decipher and stores every occurrence within its field of observation,

> "Men are ready to suffer anything from others or from heaven itself, provided that, when it comes to words, they are untouched." Giacomo Leo-pardi, *Pensieri* *(1834-37)*.

even when it is not noticed consciously. Verbal abuse is accumulated in the minds subconscious storehouse and can be dispersed and discharged with little harm in modest quantities. However, when we are consistently bombarded by abuse, unkind words, spitefulness, vindictiveness and callousness this negative energy turns inwards and manifests in a wide range of physical maladies from migraines to cancer. One particular woman underwent fourteen major operations for reoccurring cancers and cysts due directly to the physical and verbal abuse she endured from her bullyboy alcoholic husband. The day she finally gave up and left him she regained her health and the growths ceased.

Conversely, our libraries carry countless books expounding the value of encouraging words of praise, not only in psychotherapy but in salesmanship, politics, business and every conceivable type of human interaction. It remains a remarkable human oversight that such a powerfully destructive weapon as speech should be used with such disregard for the human suffering it can cause when unleashed without consideration of its effect on our fellow man.

*Judge not, that ye be not judged*! Matthew 7:1

## Chapter 10

# The Question Of Karma

*Karma: The principle of retributive justice determining a persons state of life, and the state of his reincarnations, as the effects of his past deeds.*
Collins Concise English Dictionary.

Some illness and maladies we choose to bring with us at birth, collected over many previous lives and imprinted in our consciousness. These are known as karmic diseases. From the house files one case is memorable.

Her diagnosis was every woman's nightmare! Rosa had a huge malignant tumour in her uterus. She looked as if she was four months pregnant. The doctors told her she required an immediate operation; a total hysterectomy, an operation from which she had little chance of survival. That blanket of hopelessness only the terminally ill can relate to dampened her life to the point of despair. She was in constant haemorrhage and weighed less than thirty six kilos.

She read about the healer, Joao Teixeira De Farier in a newspaper article. With little alternative hope of survival she took the long twenty four hour bus ride from her home to the House of Dom Inacio in Abadiania.

The morning sun gently warmed the crisp mountain air as she stepped down from the bus. People were quietly assembling in the entrance hall of the centre. Dressed in white shirt and slacks as she was advised, she moved to the front of the crowd. As she waited she watched the healer miraculously remove tumours from other patients and her hopes soared but, when her turn finally came, she was devastated by his first words: *"My child*

113

*I can do little for you,"* he said with deep compassion in his eyes, *"I can only relieve you a little, the rest is up to you. If you offer yourself to charity work helping others, while you work on improving your faith, you might recover."* Rosa's cancer was the result of a karmic debt which she probably earned from some immoral behaviour in a previous life.

Rosa immediately began to repay her debt by serving the sick. She volunteered to work in the house and the moment she started her condition began to improve. The more she dressed wounds and attended to the sick and mentally ill the more her own health improved. Eventually her cancer disappeared, she put on weight and, at the time of writing, was enjoying perfect health. She chose to stay on at the house and has dedicated the past seventeen years to service in the Casa de Dom Inacio. Rosa was fortunate to meet Joao and learn from the Entity how she could pay her karmic debt in this life.

Karmic debt is the means by which we pay for or clear our wrong-doings so that we, our soul or spirit, may be elevated to a higher vibrational plane after death. It is a necessary cleansing for the soul to be able to elevate to ultimate perfection. Karmic debt is something we cannot escape. It is a result of the Universal Law of Cause and Effect. If we continue to do bad things, as some people do, the spirit will degenerate to a sick and unhappy state. If we live our lives according to the universal principles of integrity, charity, honesty, love, tolerance and compassion we will have few, if any, debts to pay and eventually complete our reincarnation cycles on the earth plane. Our elevation then continues in the spirit dimension.

> "...understand man's psychic capabilities as a part of one's daily life. All events of one's life...as they relate to the activity of the soul would lead one to see all events of life - even illness - as a necessary learning experience as man passes through time and space." William A McGarey, *Edgar Cayce on Healing*.

Illness is the great leveller of all men. It does not matter who you are or what money or power you possess, sickness – especially incurable sickness – reduces us all to a state of physical and emotional helplessness. According to the entities of Joao, there are many causes of illness, one of which is karmic debt.

These diseases or afflictions are not of any specific type but they are of a single origin; the karmic correction of wrongs committed in past and current lives. The record is imprinted in the superconscious layers of memory and carried in the soul which brings with it the debt and the disease or malady it chooses to endure when it is reincarnated. The infliction may be immediately apparent as in the case of birth defects or deformity or they may develop at any time in the life cycle. Karmic illness brought from a previous life cannot be cured except by way of repayment of the debt, in like manner to the way it was indebted, by personal suffering in the manner in which the debt was incurred or it can be paid by unselfish service to mankind. The ultimate aim is awareness, learning and thus a cleansing of the soul.

Karmic debt might seem at first a discouraging thought but there is another law which says that free-will is always stronger than pre-ordained destiny. No soul is ever so encumbered with debt that it must pay forever - there are releases. One lifetime of selfless sacrifice for the welfare of others might equal five or six sterile existences where the soul stood still. This is called The Law of Grace. Whatever laws you broke, you broke of your own free will. You alone chose where you are at this moment. According to Edgar Casey, the sleeping prophet, help is only as far away as the will to put things right: *"A soul has but to acknowledge by its penitence that it has gone astray, and help would be forthcoming in exact proportion to its sincerity"*. To imagine that you are the victim of a vengeful Creator who demands repayment to satisfy some half baked whim is why the hell-fire doctrines of original sin have failed to endure. The Creator is not a vengeful God, karma is simply the means of satisfying the Universal Law of Cause and Effect.

Surprisingly, of the number of people who come to Abadiania for healing, only an infinitely small percentage carry an incurable karmic debt. Of these, some can be eased by Joao and the entities and assisted to cure themselves. In February 1996 a young man came before Joao in a wheelchair. "*You have chosen to clear a karmic debt, my son*", he said, "*I cannot help you now but we can work together and in time you will walk again.*" The young man began helping others by making woven carry-bags for the sick to carry home their herbs. Every week he received a treatment from the entity and in time the debt will be repaid and he will walk again.

### Let Him Die - It's Gods Will.

Invariably there arises the question of "*God's Will*". One hears the expression about someone who is gravely ill: "*It must be God's Will, so let him die*". Obviously it is not they who are ill! Unfortunately these people must have a very fearful opinion of a spiteful and vengeful God. It is more realistic to think of the Creator as the ultimate in caring and compassion. But ultimately God can only do so much, it is up to each of us to help ourselves as much as possible. All too often it is seen in the house, after the entities operate, some people fail to change their life-style only to redevelop the same illness. Here is a well known story to illustrate the point:

During a deluge of heavy rain a local priest was advised by the police to evacuate his church but he refused, saying that he believed God would save him. The rain continued and the priest was forced to climb onto the roof. A rescue boat came by and urged the priest to get in. He refused, saying God would protect him. When the water rose so far that he was forced to cling to the steeple a rescue boat was sent with the bishop who pleaded with the priest to evacuate. He refused, still believing God would intervene at the last moment.

The priest was swept away in the flood and ultimately arrived in heaven. He immediately confronted St.Peter and complained that he waited for God to save him but, to his disappointment, he was left to perish. St.Peter hurried away to consult with God and when he returned he said: "We did all we could to help you, we sent the police, the rescue squad and even the bishop but you wouldn't get into the boat!"

The moral of the story is that we are ultimately responsible for our own lives and if we abuse our bodies and err from our soul's good intent, eventually we must elect to correct the imbalance. But to suggest that all efforts to heal a desperately ill person should be ceased because it is 'God's will' is not only naive, it is ignorant. That is not to say that some illnesses are not 'cleansing' and need to run their course, but such cases will result in restored health unless the soul chooses otherwise in an effort to correct some predetermined imbalance. Under the Law of Self Determination our free will extends to decisions as to the future quality of life we choose to lead.

## Chapter 11
## Scientific Observations

*Science is really the statement of a value system. What it calls its "objective" stance toward reality - detachment, analysis, prediction and control - is actually a statement of values. It is a bias in favour of a certain attitude toward knowledge.*
Henry Reed,. Edgar Casey Modern Prophet.

Almost all of the scientists who come to test Joao and his paranormal methods arrive with their white coats of bias and scepticism. Some leave confused, but none leave with their scepticism intact.

Many medical doctors come to Abadiania, either openly or covertly. Some come to scoff, some determined to prove the man a charlatan, others to be healed of their own afflictions, most go away completely convinced that he is a true phenomenon of medicine. The consensus is that Joao is quite unbelievable and yet the cold empirical evidence of the success of his operations leaves them no choice other than believing the unbelievable - that he is an authentic paranormal phenomenon of medicine.

Animosity by some of the medical profession is understandable, not just from the point of view of competition, but also pride. The educational requirements for doctors in Brazil are as strenuous as they are in the United States, with pre-med, medical school, internship and residency - all requiring gross investment of time and money. For a country-born man of humble origins to attract such acclaim from internationally prominent citizens and dignitaries might naturally sting their professional pride. But those of the medical profession who look beyond their resentment usually find themselves in awe of what their eyes see but their minds grapple to comprehend.

Joao has been the study of many foreign scientific teams from Russia, Germany, U.S.A., Japan and France. He always encourages research into his healing abilities in the hope that medical science can utilise some of the knowledge in the treatment of mankind's illnesses. Sadly, despite the intensity and success of these studies, little of the gathered knowledge is utilised in western medicine.

### The U.B.M Studies.

The most extensive and intense study was conducted by the faculty of Clinical Bio-physics from the University of Dr.Bezerro de Menezes. The university sponsored a full time two year study team, headed by Doctor A.Arlete Savaris who obverved Joao and the activities of the centre for two years and studied Joao's every action; testing, probing, comparing pre and post operative results and scientifically compiling the data which was finally presented in 1995 as a formidable scientific book, *Curas Paranormais Realizadas por Joao de Farias*, now available to the public from the university or the centre. There has possibly never been a more intense study of this type of medically oriented paranormal phenomena. Unfortunately it has never been translated into English. A precis of the conclusion to this thesis by Dr Savaris is translated here as best as possible. In it she states the following:

*"The purpose of this thesis was to collect and collate all available data on the paranormal healing performed by Joao Teixeira de Faria, a phenomenal talent of this unorthodox science. It was observed that the people who sought cures returned home alleviated of their pain and desperation as if they had become new people. From then on they*

*also showed concern for other people, seeking ways to help others (a change in their spiritual and humanitarian attitude).*

Human beings are complex, as are their diseases and their fears, so it is difficult to understand what happens in that brief moment when they submit themselves to paranormal healing. Some physicists affirm that matter is not formed of basic building blocks but that the universe is an inseparable set where exists a web of probabilities that interact and interlace themselves. Some works show that the universe has emerged from this set. They show that, existing in several parts of the whole, we can enter into a state of holistic being and absorb healing energies from the universe to instantly heal anybody in any place. Certain healers can do this by funding themselves from this universal force and connecting themselves to both the force and to the patient. It is possible that this healing force may be a phase of harmony of our quantum waves.

"Most physicians recognise that the mysteries of the body and its functions are truly beyond our present comprehension and that a spiritual being manifesting as a physical body must be a strange entity indeed. Our knowledge today is insufficient at best, and degrees (only) give us the legal right to exercise that knowledge gained in our studies." William McGarey, *Edgar Cayce on Healing.*

According to Newton's theory of separate parts it is possible with positive energy to provoke quantic leaps. If we humans are energy fields, then we can donate it (energy) as well as receive it. In a current of higher consciousness it may be possible to perform fantastic healings, and if this occurs with spiritual assistance it will add to the result.

The energy pattern of the healer (Joao) differs from other people due to the way he 'stereoises' his energies with an unquestionable spiritual link, connecting the man to his essence, (in an existence) where there are no limits or frontiers (of time or space).

Healing consciousness has many origins. If Jesus gave importance to healing with his deciples and apostles, I conclude that healing is not a privilege of religions but of human beings. Healing is only a practical application of a basic Christian principal.

The first doctors, often looked upon as witches, considered that the physical, emotional and spiritual parts were inseparable. They made use of natural plants to prepare formulas in an intimate relationship between man and nature.

Disease can be the result of a state of disharmony between body, mind and soul but man, through his reluctance to accept the responsibility for his own state of health, prefers to blame viruses or other outside influences. Studies indicate that most diseases originate in the esoterical body due to wrong use of personal energies (anger, frustration, fear, anxiety, hate and jealousy).

The act of healing is as old as disease itself, but only recently there has been considerable interest by scientists in the field of paranormal healing whose methods and results conflict with the restrictive education of researchers and scientists. A great deal more research needs to be done into the healing methods and techniques of our ancestors.

Medicine of the future cannot be based solely on paranormal healing, ignoring the superb advancement and sophisticated development of modern medicine, but there should be an acceptance of these alternative methods of healing that have clearly demonstrated such positive results. The combination of the two can give rise to the medicine of the future, with the ability to overcome all diseases; physical, spiritual and mental.

*Hopefully, in the near future, there will be union between physics, medicine and paranormal healing. There is no magic, no mystery. The energy is, in the last analysis, the energy that exists within us all."*

### *Studies of Spiritual Surgery - Tests by Faculty of Medicine, Federal University de Juis de Fora. Minas Gerias, Brazil.*

Report by Alexander Moreira de Almeida, Tatiana Moreira de Almeida and Angela Maria Gollner as reported in the magazine O IDEAL;

"Notwithstanding the fact that Spiritual Surgery has been lacking in serious research from a scientific viewpoint, it has greatly interested the media and the public in general. It is clearly noticeable that most of the opinions expressed on the subject in newspapers, television and magazines are expressed from a preconceived point of view, either favourable or unfavourable according to the individual's conviction.

According to Marlene Nobre, president of the Brazilian Spiritistic-Medical Association, many medium healers are looked upon with reservation due to the lack of deeper studies on the subject.

Notwithstanding the fact that thousands of people in the world are healed in this unorthodox way, many researchers refuse to study the matter, assuming that it is nothing but fraud. That the cuts are tricks, the blood only dye and the fragments extracted from patients are of animal origin. Unfortunately this opinion is reinforced by those spiritual surgeons, the world over, who refuse to allow the removal of tissue for scientific examination.

In our study we sought the assistance of the Pathology Department of the University Hospital. Our aim was to establish whether these phenomena are frauds or of a positive nature requiring further studies. We chose, as our subject, the medium from Goiana, Joao Teixeira de Faria, who works in the town of Abadiania, because he treats over 1000 people per day and is constantly in the media for treating internationally famous people.

The medium has only an elementary schooling, he is the owner of a ranch in Anapolis and he provides treatment (free of charge) in a centre which does not bear a spirititist title. He has a strong and decisive personality but each of the spirits he incorporates manifest their own personality, some kind, some rude and some firm.

It was observed that groups arrived every Wednesday, Thursday and Friday from every part of Brazil. They received treatment for various ailments by one or more spirit entities, manifesting themselves in Joao Teixeira, either by natural herbs or by spiritual surgery if required.

"Does it not give one the feeling that we are on the threshold of finding new ways (or are they regained from the records of antiquity?) to bring healing to the body, hope to the mind, and direction to the spirit of man on earth?" Mary Ellen Carter, Hugh Lynne Cayce, *Edgar Cayce on Prophesy*.

According to a statement by the centre, there is no need for visible surgery (with incisions) as all treatment can be done by invisible surgery (an operation effected through the spiritual body). The choice is the patient's. We decided to study the visible surgery, carried out before the waiting crowds. We filmed and photographed a series of operations, the patients were interviewed and examined and all of the organic substances were collected and removed for pathological testing at the university.

None of the patients received any form of anaesthetic and only one of them said they felt a mild form of pain during the operation. The instruments used were mostly kitchen knives or bistoury (surgical knife). No form of antiseptic was observed.

We observed a series of operations including; scraping the eye cornea, the introduction of scissors-shaped tweezers tipped with cotton wool into the nasal cavity, the extraction of teeth, breast surgery and abdominal surgery and the surgical removal of a lymphoma (benign tumour) weighing 120 grams from a patient's back.

Our conclusions firmly uphold that the surgery is genuine. The pathological tests reveal that the removed substances are compatible with their origins and that they are human tissues.

*We contend that further studies are urgently needed to deepen our knowledge of this subject. In particular the following should be investigated; the lack of pain during physical surgery even without anaesthesia, and the absence of asepsis. It is our recommendation that science should urgently devote more serious research into this matter that could effect the life of millions throughout the world."*

### The American Tests.

In 1992 Joao willingly agreed to make himself available for examination at a special congress of international doctors organised by Canadian and American scientists held in Caldas Novas, Goias.

The results were positively conclusive and many of the sceptics who came to prove him false left convinced of his capabilities but bewildered as to what to do with the data. It is difficult enough for a scientifically trained mind to comprehend how he is able to perform such amazing operations, but it is humbling indeed to observe an uneducated man of no medical experience whatsoever, perform more successful operations in a single day than most major university medical centres would see in a month!

### Aura Measurements.

It is always difficult for science to study and examine paranormal phenomena because science needs to observe and measure the action in progress. This is rather difficult when the action is provided by spirit. However, there are things that can be measured, such as the power of Joao's bio-energy field, or aura, during incorporation and in his normal state and then compared to a normal human aura.

This series of tests, carried out on 9th May 1987 by scientist Lloyd Youngblood, President of American Society of Downsers, showed the strength and size of Joao's bio-energy field to be twelve times the normal human health aura before incorporation and an incredible *twenty times* the normal human health aura when he incorporated the spirit of Dr. Oswaldo Cruz. The measurement recordings were:

| | |
|---|---|
| Normal human health aura.............. | 0.45 metres |
| Joao's normal health aura ............. | 6.12 metres |
| Joao's Incorporated health aura...... | **9.14 metres** |
| Normal human ethereal (spiritual) aura....... | 0.04 metres |
| Joao's ethereal (spiritual) aura ................... | 0.95 metres |
| Joao Incorporated ethereal aura............ | **13.71 metres** |

Scientists by their very nature are sceptical and, even when they observe a result, need to find a logical connection between the cause and the effect. This is not always possible so they are obliged to compare the state of the subject before treatment and observe the post treatment results. Here there is no conflict. No doubt. There are countless cases of 'before' and 'after' to study and thousands of grateful recipients who are willing to testify. One such indisputable case is that of a young 23 year old man, himself a doctor of medicine.

### Brain Tumour Testimonial Video.

The recently graduated Dr. Klaun of Minera Gerias became gravely ill when he developed a 4cm. wide brain tumour. His family sought the best advice the world had to offer. They took him to America and engaged the three best specialists in their respective fields - neurology, cancer and surgery. The prognosis was not good; less than a fifty percent chance of surviving the operation and only a twenty percent chance of living a normal life if he lived through it. The best he could expect is a modest extension of his life, probably as a paraplegic.

The family had little to lose so they sought an alternative answer. They knew of Joao because the young man's father, himself a doctor, worked within the Ministry for Health in the Brazilian government and had cause to receive objections from medical associations as well as letters of praise about the "the healer from Abadiania". They consulted with Joao who assured them that a spirit operation was quite feasible and a total recovery was more than just a possibility.

In November 1994 he came to the house with his father and two of the doctors who diagnosed the tumour. He was placed in the intensive operations room and went into a coma for three days during which he was operated on by spirit. For three days and nights his body all but shut down physical functions - no food, no eliminations, no movement. When he finally awoke on the third day he was advised to have another X-ray. The enormous tumour had completely disappeared. The before and after X-rays and the critical observations of such qualified medical practitioners constituted a medically observed phenomena. All were prepared to participate in a statement which verified the pre operation and post operation conditions. On 15th November 1994 a testimonial video was produced before hundreds of people in which each doctor and the patient testified to their observations and the successful result:

Firstly the radiologist showed the pre-operation X-rays and made his statement; in his opinion there was no chance of survival by normal surgery.

Then the young doctor made his own statement: *"I was in the USA for two months under medical observation. I was in hospital with the best available medical doctors."* he said.

127

When the interviewer asked what the reaction was of these specialist after the spirit operation, he replied; *"They were stunned that the X-rays showed no sign of any surgical cut to access the tumour and that I was in such remarkably good health."*

A statement was then made by Dr. Maureso de Veta of the Brazilian Ministry of Health after examining the specialist reports and the X-rays. He gave his professional opinion of the inoperability of the tumour and declared that the tumour was indeed gone, without any sign of surgical entry to the skull. Today, two and a half years later, he is healthy, without any sign of the cancer. This video testimony is available from the centre achieves.

### A Difficult Task

Facing the medical scientists who come to observe, examine, test and record is a formidable task. Where does one begin? There is so much to evaluate and interpret:

1. Firstly there is the lack of pre-operative preparation. The conscious patients are completely calm, relaxed, and indicate no fear whatsoever, yet they have received neither tranquillisers nor anaesthesia. They remain totally impassive without expression of anxiety or muscular tension, even though the operations performed on them are nothing less than traumatic under normal circumstances.

2. There is very little blood from any surgery. Almost nothing from incisions that would normally bleed profusely.

3. The instruments used are sterile but Joao will frequently insert his bare fingers into the incision. There should be massive post-operative infection but there has never been a reported case of septicaemia in the more than thirty years of operations.

4. Many of the surgical routines observed cannot be performed even by highly trained surgeons.

5. Some of the treatments defy current medical understanding. He performs twenty eight different operations on various parts of the body by inserting scissors-like clamps into the nostril and twisting them, like winding a grandfather clock. In one observed case this technique was used to rejoin six compound fractures in a man's feet. The man came into the centre on knee pads and walked out on his reassembled feet! He went back to work within a week. And yet there is evidence in the West that may substantiate such treatment: Newsweek magazine (Nov 8, 1971) reported that researchers at University of Pennsylvania had successfully used direct pulsating electrical current to accelerate the rate of healing of a patient with a bone fracture. This may give a hint at how Joao might speed the healing using a divine energy, but it does nothing to explain how the six fractures realigned themselves or how the cure relates to the method used.

6. Similarly, his operations through the eye defy logic. Apart from the removal of cataracts and tumours from the eye itself with an unsterilized kitchen knife, he also performs numerous operations throughout the body by scrapping the knife across the eyeball - an excruciatingly painful procedure under normal circumstances. His patients show little sign of discomfort. It has been reported by observing doctors that a strange blue light can be seen emanating from the tip of the knife, but find the occurrence quite unexplainable.

7. Then there is the phenomenon of invisible operations. No one physically touches the patient! They simply sit in meditation focusing on their problem. Joao-in-entity enters the room and declares; *"In the name of Jesus Christ you are all operated"*. Scientific observers can only select patients who have recognisable pre-operative conditions, preferably with X-rays, and examine them after the operation procedure. They always report baffling evidence of internal operations and all signs of the malady, be it tumour, cyst, gallstone etc., gone.

8. As if to defy their scientific logic, Joao has been observed to remove a cancer from the stomach of an eighty year old woman by simply blowing on the back of her head! This was done just to demonstrate that it is not _he_ who is operating, but _spirit_. He could just as easily have stood on his head to achieve the same result.

### The Schubert Experiments.

In December 1984 German scientist Dr. Klause Schubert, co-ordinated a joint investigation at the University of Friburg, Alemanha in Rio de Janeiro, attended by Sr. Prof. Dr. Bender of the Institute of Parapsychology of Rio de Janeiro, Sr. Prof. Mario Amaral Machado, Sr. Geraldo dos Santos Sarti and Dr. Horta Santos. Not all of these eminent scientists were believers but at the end of the experiments they were all unanimous in their belief that *Joao was indeed a true paranormal medical phenomenon*. A high quality documentary film was made of the teams examinations and tests of both invisible and visible operations. This film, *Medium Joao de Deus,* was studied by many institutions in Germany and aired on German prime time television.

Dr Schubert concluded his investigation with the statement that he was honoured to have been able to meet and observe this *"truly remarkable man"*.

### Herbs and Water.

A large part of the treatment process at the centre is achieved by medicinal herbs which are prescribed by the entities and prepared by the house pharmacists. There is a small charge of US$5 per bottle and as many as six bottles may be prescribed.

This modest charge barely covers the cost of production of the complex mixtures which contain up to one hundred and sixty different herbs.

Joao received instruction in the collection and preparation of the herbs from an indigenous entity Cavoclo Gentile when, as a young man, he was travelling through a remote inland area of Brazil. He was destitute, alone and hungry. Taking shelter in a small fazenda (farm), he treated the local people who, in return for healing and spiritual advice, provided him with eggs, chickens and rice.

These people had little money to buy pharmaceuticals so Joao sought the help of his entities. He was directed to the forest where he received instruction on which herbs to select and the method of preparation for each type of ailment. He has since taught his pharmacists to gather and prepare the medicines which form a large part of the healing treatments. During a single visit to Colatina in January 1996, they dispensed over fifteen thousand bottles of herbal medicines in less than three days; a formidable logistics exercise to transport such a large quantity from Abadiania.

The centre also sells treated water which is being recommended more and more frequently for its medicinal and curative value. It has long been recognised by scientists that there are many different types of water on our planet, some of them are extraordinarily therapeutic. According to an article in the January 1995 issue of the scientific magazine Nexus, water is the *"new fountain of youth"*. The Nobel laureate, Szent-Gyorgyi who discovered vitamin C, calls water *"the mother and matrix of life.* We tend to ignore it and look elsewhere for the magic bullet or the secret nutrient that will increase health and vigour and extend life-span."* All the symptoms of ageing are associated with free-radical oxidative damage. There is much more to tissue hydration than drinking ordinary water. Tissue water is as different from ordinary water as milk is from apple juice.

Dr Coanda, the father of the jet aeroplane, spent sixty years studying water and its medicinal effects. He said that the human body is over seventy per cent water and the brain is ninety per cent water. Certain water, which he called "anomalous water", contains within it's structure the secret to reversing the ageing process. He travelled the world extensively and found five places that contained "anomalous water". Two of these places included Hunza land in northern Pakistan and the Vilcabamba in Equador. It has fascinated anthropologists that people who live in these areas tend to remain healthy and disease-free well beyond the age of 100 years.

After ten years of experiments, research scientists Patrick and Gael Flanagan, reproduced Coanda's anomalous water which contained different properties to ordinary water; surface tension, viscosity, heat capacity and free energy, as well as an increased quantity of negatively ionised hydrogen atoms. They duplicated a "colloidal mineral cluster" only found in these Hunza-type waters. Mineral clusters of this tiny size have unusual properties not found in any other type of matter. Electrons can travel all over the surface of the mineral instead of being confined to localised areas like electrons found in ordinary colloids. These "electron clouds" form a negative electrical charge that attracts and organises water molecules into a liquid crystal structure.

This structure resembles the water found in the living system rather than that in ordinary or mineral waters. When we drink ordinary water we have to convert it to cellular water before the body can use it. If it cannot convert it to cellar water, it will pass through our bodies and leave our cells partially dehydrated. The tiny mineral clusters found in Hunza-type water resemble those found in living systems and will energise practically all nutrients with which they come in contact.

Additionally, studies show that our bodies store hydrogen in tissue. As we age, hydrogen depletion may lead to many ageing symptoms; chronic fatigue, depression, hormone imbalances, stiffness and inflexibility. It is hydrogen that protects our cells from oxidative free-radical damage and provides energy to the cells when it is burned by oxygen. Hydrogen is the ultimate anti-oxidant. Consumption of Hunza-type water with its superior distribution system may provide negatively charged hydrogen ions, acting as the perfect free-radical scavenger. It would also be used in the production of ATP, the biological battery which supplies the energy needs of the human body. The purpose of eating food is to create ATP.

Scientifically then, it is recognised that certain waters are amongst the most important substances to human health and vitality. It is not surprising that the entities should be drawing on their universal knowledge to provide us with a medicinal water for our improved health. There have been scientific studies made of the Abadiania water in which scientists state there was a *"definite change in its chemical composition after 'fluidation' (a name used to describe the change in chemical composition) by Joao-in entity"*. Its therapeutic benefits are acclaimed by thousands who return frequently to Abadiania to spend a few days in the spiritual atmosphere and to take away with them their treated water.

Joao is always willing to make himself available for examination or observation by genuine researchers in his desire for the world to understand the connection between man, his spirit and his Creator. Unfortunately all too often the scientists' only objective is to try to expose him as a charlatan. Unable to do so they dismiss it as paranormal and of little use in their scientific world. Unfortunately Joao will pass on some day and the opportunity to utilise his knowledge and his methods will pass with him. It will be a sorry loss for mankind.

Further research has revealed the wonderful scientific work done by Dr Bernard Grad, a Canadian scientist who stringently tested the effects that spiritual healers have on the human body, plant growth and water. In the 1960's he conducted a series of carefully controlled tests involving the effects of healer-energized water. The results concluded that healer treated water underwent measurable cellular changes: a disruption to its hydrogen bonding, a molecular 'charge' and a decrease in its surface tension. Dr Grad also proved that energy was both positive and negative depending on the attitude of the energizer; water energized by spiritual healers always produced strong positive growth in laboratory controlled plants whilst water energized by a manic depressive produced stunted growth and poor yields.

The prescribed herbs, as stated elsewhere, are now produced in dry powder capsules so that Joao is better able to transport them to other centres in cities throughout Brazil. This lighter more portable form is also more convenient for the many foreigners who now find their way to the Casa de Dom Inacio.

### Chapter 12

## Taking Miracles To The World

A man's feet must be planted in his country, but his eyes should survey
the world.
George Santayana, The Life of Reason: Reason in Society (1905-06).

Joao is willing to travel anywhere in the world to heal the sick
but there are some difficulties particular to him beyond any
normal restriction that might restrain even the most prominent
dignitary.

There are the usual permissions from governments, police
and authorities, including a tacit approval from those ever-
threatening factions within the medical profession and, in some
countries, the ecclastical authorities. Then there is the need for
crowd control and personal security, not necessarily because of
deliberate threats to Joao personally but because of the vast
numbers of people seeking his help who follow him where ever
he goes.

There must be a venue big enough to accommodate the
thousands who flock to be treated; it must be safe, preferably
privately owned so that disagreeable factions cannot implement
some right of tenure to interrupt the proceedings. Sports stadi-
ums, schools, gymnasiums or associations are preferred for their
size and charitable attitudes.

The question of costs is complicated by lack of compensa-
tion. Someone must pay for at least eight members of his team
- mediums, lawyers, administrators, Joao and his wife - airfares,
hotels, a security team and transportation. But philanthropical
sponsors cannot recoup their financial outlays by direct charges

or commercial sponsorship. Joao cannot request payment for his work and this applies also to his sponsors.

Finally, Joao does not like to neglect his responsibilities in Brazil to provide a weekly service on Wednesday, Thursday and Friday at Abadiania to those who travel thousands of kilometres to receive his cures. Thus, if possible, he tries to complete his travel in four days to be back in time for the weekly session.

Despite these obstacles he has managed international trips to Bolivia, USA, Argentina, Paraguay, Portugal, and Peru where he has been invited five times. Not all of them were meant to be healing trips; during a short holiday in Portugal he became so restless that he felt compelled to offer his services to the public. His presence had been announced by the press and the demand for his work, combined with his restlessness, resulted in a series of sessions held in the premises of the Lisbon Association for the Blind. Hundreds queued for healings and those of the media who came to scoff were left incredulous by the amazing miracles they witnessed. As a result there was the usual pressure from the medical association which almost resulted in him being jailed. It was avoided in Portugal but in Peru, under charges laid by the Peruvian Medical Association, he was arrested and incarcerated.

In April 1991, Joao and a party of thirty mediums, lawyers, interpreters and nurses was sponsored for his first trip to Lima, Peru by councillor Luis Rosello, who was previously healed of a serious cardiac problem. The Peruvian medical association pulled out all guns; releasing television statements that he was a hoax and pursuing him vigorously through the legal system. Joao was finally arrested and thrown in jail. Public outcry and a closer look at his healing work, possibly with pressure from the fourteen medical doctors who received his help for their own afflictions, finally convinced the association to withdraw the charges and even issue a statement that he was authentic. Joao immediately returned to curing the sick.

At this time there was a serious and widespread outbreak of cholera in Peru. There is no way of evaluating how many cholera victims were treated by Joao but Mr Segundo Mota, who travelled with him, believes that more than half of those who came for healing were afflicted with the disease. So many Peruvians sought his help that it was necessary to hire the local sports stadium. According to a report by the agency of France Press, during his fifteen days he healed over 20,000 people including the President of Peru, Alberto Fujinori and his son: *"There was the usual throwing away of crutches, blind people recovering their sight and the extraction of tumours"*. The president was treated for atrophy of his hands and his son for a serious mental disorder. In gratitude the president awarded him with a Medal of Honor.

A few weeks after his return to Abadiania three Peruvians turned up at the centre with cholera. They had been travelling for two weeks to get there and reported that they knew of more than twenty others on the way. The state Secretary of Health, Mr Ernesto Marinho, went on tour to the centre to investigate the possibility of contamination but was assured by Joao that he could cure the cases and there would be no cause for concern.

Detailed recording of his international trips is always difficult because there is such heavy demand upon the healer and his staff. A rare insight into the multitude of problems and the subsequent strain on all party members, especially Joao, were recorded during a trip to Peru in January 1994 by Judge Jose Liberato Costa Povoa in his book, *Joao de Deus, Phenominon de Abadiania.*

The trip was planned to visit Puno, a city of 400,000 inhabitants, 1000 km. from the capital Lima. Located on the shores of Lake Titicaca, 3840 metres above sea level, where just breathing was a discomfort. The high altitude was exacerbated by constant rain and biting cold, with temperatures seldom rising above eight degrees Celsius.

The thousands of sick and crippled who came to see him waited, some of them for two nights, in these intolerable conditions. Joao and his team worked under extraordinarily difficult circumstances but, as he had accepted the invitation to visit this remote region because of the extreme poverty and the difficult life of the people, he put aside his personal discomfort in his determination to provide help to as many people as was possible in the limited time.

Judge Povoa reports that the crowds gathered at each airport on the way to Puno. Landing initially in Lima at daybreak, they were shocked to see the airport was teeming with people waiting in the early morning cold to catch a glimpse of the medium. The media was out in force and it was an hour before the group of seven could make their way to the hotel to rest until the evening departure for Arequipa, an intermediate landing en route to Puno. To their surprise this airport also was crowded with people hopeful of seeing Joao de Deus. Finally they landed at Juliaca, completing the forty-five kilometre journey by road to the high mountain city of Puno.

At Juliaca the authorities were prepared with a large security force to handle the crowds and any unexpected action by terrorists, who might use the opportunity to bring media attention to their activities. As an indication of the importance the Peruvians placed on a visit by Joao, an elite force of one hundred men were selected from both the army and the police force, headed by two generals; General of the Peruvian Army, Gen. Luis Paz Cardenas and Gen. Luniciano Cesar Ramirez Vinatea of the Peruvian Police Force. *"The Hotel dos Turistas was under 24 hour guard from terrorists and the daily invasion of people that gathered in the hope of a blessing or a cure."* reported Liberato Povoa. *"The passage of Joao through the streets to the healing venue at The Puno Shooting Club was protected by full security. It would have been impossible for him to walk unharmed through the sea of people. They would have fought to touch him or tear pieces from his clothing exposing him to great physical risk,"* he added. The procession was headed by Gen. Ramirez personally, heralded by the wail of police sirens.

The toll that this type of visit takes on Joao is revealed in the observations by Judge Povoa who worked closely with the medium as an interpreter: *"Although work began at 8 am each day there was no scheduled finishing time, only when the last patient was attended to, often far into the night, did he cease. On our return to the hotel, accompanied by the security forces, we were always confronted with a large crowd. Joao insisted on helping them one by one, often retiring around two in the morning, only to rise at six to begin again. At the end of each day we were exhausted, but I was particularly impressed by Joao's stamina; beginning each day with only a glass of Mamao (Papaya) juice and eating nothing all day until very late at night, when he ate only a small meal."*

Prompted by television and newspaper reports of the visit, caravans of people made their way to Puno from the surrounding provinces, Cusco, Iquitos, Arequipa as well as from neighbouring countries Chile and Venezuela. As always, a swarm of reporters descended on the city to interview the medium.

In five days it is estimated that over 20,000 people were treated including over 1,000 visible and invisible operations, all under the watchful eyes of inspectors from the Ministerio Publico and the Medical Association. *"It is difficult"*, writes Povoa, *"to select particularly spectacular healings. There were so many of them."* But the ones that remain prominent in his mind include the following:

"I particularly remember a young girl of 13 or 14, a dancer belonging to a folk dance group from Cusco, who dragged herself in on crutches. She was the victim of a car accident which left her paralysed from the waist down. Joao massaged her legs and then said positively: 'Walk.... you are healed!' Under incredulous eyes she emerged from the crowd and symbolically threw her crutches away. She walked with difficulty at first but a little later, with encouraging applause from the crowd, she was walking almost normally. During interviews by the press and TV reporters her face was flooded with tears of gratitude."

A special request was made by Gen. Cardenas for Joao to attend to the needs of approximately 1,000 relatives of army personnel. Amongst these patients was a young boy, well known in Puno because he was the son of a prominent military family, who was almost paralysed by an unknown illness. He could only walk with extreme difficulty with the aid of crutches. *"Very few who knew him believed he could be cured,"* reports Povoa, *"because he had been under extensive treatment by physiotherapists and orthopaedists without results. When the crutches were taken away from him and he began to walk the crowd stared in disbelief, and I observed two tears roll gently down the hardened face of Gen. Cardenas."*

*"On the second last day,"* the learned judge writes, *"an old man came with his relatives who said he had been totally deaf for many years. Joao placed his palms over both ears and then asked a relative to stand away behind him and call his name in a modest voice. When he heard his name called the old man turned to answer. He was last seen being lead from the hall with tears streaming down his face."*

"Another remarkable case was that of Commander Mario Garcia Noe of the National Peruvian Police. He was the victim of a terrorist attack and his spinal cord had been injured which left him paralysed from the waist down. By the time we left for

Lima Commander Mario was standing on his legs and could walk with help. He was given hope for a full recovery."

During the second last day the "fluidified" water ran out and stocks had to be rushed in from Arequipa, 350 kkilometres away. During the last day people bought their own water in plastic bottles and even plastic bags for Joao to "fluidate". *"Sometimes,"* said Povoa, *"this water was dirty and looked as if it had been collected from the street puddles. This worried us very much, particularly as Puno has no sanitation and has drainage flowing directly into the streets. Peru is also a known source of cholera. It was like a miracle that there was not a single case of cholera during our entire stay in Peru".*

Apart from the problems of cold, rain, rarefied atmosphere and incredibly long hours, there were side issues which required serious consideration. During this trip a large producer of mineral water offered to sponsor another trip to the city of Arequipa with the proviso that his product be the only one used for "fluidation" and distribution at the healing venue. After due consideration, Joao declined because of the possibility of commercial use of his name. He never accepts an invitation that might in any way imply a profit for his work. Another distraction occurred when a rumour spread that tickets were being sold for an audience with the medium. Joao was visibly upset and ceased work, threatening to return immediately to Brazil if it was true. Fortunately it was established that the rumours were false and work resumed.

On the last day in Puno Joao was presented with a march-past of the entire Provincial Peruvian Army in full dress uniform, an honour usually reserved for heads of government. The troops marched past with respect and gratitude in their eyes despite the intermittent rain and freezing conditions. It was a heart-warming gesture offered by a grateful community, one which touched Joao very deeply.

### Chapter 13

# The Lonely Path

"The first test of a truly great man is his humility."
John Ruskin, *Modern Painters*. (1840-1860).

To the thousands who turn to him for help and healing, very few realise the enormous pressure their demands place upon him, both as a human being and as a medium. Despite the endless lines of people who wait for hours to speak to him, touch him or seek his help, it is a lonely life. Even the 'children of the house', some two hundred and fifty of them, who dedicate their time and efforts to assist in the running of the centre and to provide the spiritual current, can only glimpse the effects of such consistent pressure on his personal life.

He endeavours to keep his personal problems to himself so that they do not share his pain. Out of respect, little is discussed about his private life which has been plagued with more than a fair share of sorrow. Apart from an impoverished birthright, hunger, physical abuse, frequent attempts on his life, persecution and countless incarcerations during his early life, Joao lost his first wife under horrendous circumstances and recently his close friend and nephew in a plane crash. Any one of these could cause a lesser man to turn on his Creator with scorn but to Joao they were always tests of his faith.

To imply that, because he is guided and used by such high spiritual entities, he does not need to suffer - that he never feels despair, loneliness or sadness - is quite the opposite of the reality. It is almost a multiplier effect - the greater the mission, the greater the tests and the suffering.

Accepting such a lifetask is to accept the suffering, persecutions, ridicule and the enormous responsibility. As if that were not enough he must also observe, through the eyes of his entities, the anguish of every single soul who comes before him. To trivialise the effect of this accumulated suffering of the masses would be a sorry injustice to the man. It is not uncommon to observe the disappointment and frustration he feels in the line of humanity that passes him each day.

> "No words can be said, no teaching can be taught that will relieve spiritual travellers from the necessity of picking their own ways, working out with effort and anxiety their own paths through the unique circumstances of their own lives toward the identification of their individual selves with God."
> M. Scott Peck, *The Road Less Travelled.*

One young woman faced him for a second time. Joao-in-entity stared into her eyes and shook his head in disgust. *"No, my daughter,"* he said with visible frustration, *"You have scorned my work and treated me with disrespect. I treated you two months ago but you threw away the medicine and ridiculed my treatment. Now your condition has worsened and you want me to treat you again. I will not treat you until you learn gratitude and humility,"* he added as he symbolically laid his pen down. The woman sank to her knees and wept but Joao treated three more (grateful) patients before he finally scribbled a new prescription with a shake of his head and a sigh that came deep from within his heavy frame.

What frustration can compare with the realisation that, despite his dedication and sacrifice for those who seek his cures, many of these same recipients leave the operation room after receiving life saving cures only to light up a cigarette or return to their same old illness-forming habits?

What motivates a man to continue such a demanding mission? There is no superannuating nest egg, monetary reward or golden watch at the end of a lifetime of dedication to the relief of human suffering. It would seem his rewards are persecution, ridicule, incarceration and injustice. But if you ask him he would reply; *"This is my life's mission."* He would then add a quotation from the bible:

"This is my commandment: That ye love one another as I have loved you.

*Greater love hath no man than this, that a man lay down his life for his fellow man."* John 15.13 13

Joao has stated on many occasions that his greatest joy and satisfaction is when he is thanked by someone he and his entities have cured. If this is so, then the letters of gratitude that flood the tiny office of the centre each week from all over the world, must be a source of great happiness.

Reward comes in many forms; the dedication of his volunteer staff, the one hundred or more mediums who travel thousands of kilometres each week to sit in current. Or even the song written by the famous Brazilian singer Alberto, who was cured of a critical illness. The words say it all:

"I was desperately ill.

The medical doctors gave up

Saying there was no cure.

*A friend told me to go and see Joao.*

My salvation would be in the

House of Dom Inacio

In the midst of green pastures.

I left the house totally cured and happy

With divine hands and spiritual force

I saw Joao perform his amazing healings."


This lilting song is played every day throughout the house whenever the principal entity Dom Inacio is incorporated.

.What then is the lesson that you and I should learn from this remarkable man, his beloved entities and his dedicated staff, who give without counting the cost, whose sole purpose in life is to give freely their love and devotion to ease the suffering of their fellow man?

Apart from the running repairs they provide for our temporary home, this miraculous but clumsy carcass we call our body, they create in us an awareness; of our destiny, our purpose on this earth plane, and of our spirit origins. That this physical plane in which we dwell is subservient to, and dominated by, a vast spirit world which interacts with each of us every moment of our lives. An awareness that: *"As we sow, So shall we reap"*. That ultimately, through love and respect, caring and compassion we will return 'home'.

"We are not human beings having a spiritual experience. We are spiritual beings having a human experience." Pierre Teilhard de Chardin

## Chapter 14
## Case Histories

*Dedicated to those who believed, and gained a second chance at life.*

After five years of travel, covering more than three million air miles and over 100,000 road miles to research this book. In the course of personally accompanying over one thousand people and assisting more than five thousand world-wide to reach the Casa de Dom Inacio, the author has accumulated an impressive amount of feed-back. The following cases are but a selected few.

Although the success rate at the house is extraordinarily high, in the order of eighty five percent, very few healings are miraculously instant. Many factors influence the recovery rate; time for tissue to heal and cells to regenerate, adjustment in life style, change in attitude toward our fellow man and our environment, even the possibity of karmic debt. A number of visits may be required because the person might not be spiritually ready or because the illness may need to be treated in stages. Despite these provisos the files in the tiny office at Abadiania bulge with thousands of sworn testimonies and newspaper clippings that carry the news of the amazing cures of Joao de Deus:

TRIBUNA. Vitoria. Sunday 3/3/1996.
***"After a Number of Operations, Woman Walks Again.***
Before being treated by Joao de Deus, Maria de Coneicao Dalmacio was operated twice by medical doctors for a slipped disk.

'*Before this I couldn't walk a step without my crutch. Today I feel like another woman and I even managed to wash the front steps of my house!*', said Maria, a 40 year old housewife of Vitoria, Espirito Santo. '*I will never again have to use a crutch.*' she happily declared.

Victim of a slipped disk in her back, she underwent two operations by traditional surgery but was given no hope of ever walking again. In desperation she sought the help of Joao de Deus and, according to her, she was cured of her problem. '*I had two operations but every time the disk slipped again and my legs got atrophic and I was obliged to use a crutch. Although I am a minister of the Eucaristic Church and facing the disapproval of all my friends, I wanted more than anything to get back my health.*

*After having queued from seven in the morning until three in the afternoon, I entered the sick room. Joao de Deus approached, put his hands between my legs and then on my spine. Immediately after the treatment I discarded my crutch and I walked back home*'.

BRAZIL CENTRAL , 8 March 1995

**"*Mother and Son Cured.***

*Both Mrs Krug and her son were miraculously cured in the House of Dom Inacio. Alessandreo Nardes Krug, a healthy youngster of 15, suddenly began to feel excruciating pain in the legs which left him paralysed and confined to a wheelchair. He underwent extensive allopathic medicinal treatments but the doctors finally admitted that it could be one of many things including Osteoporosis, Multiple Sclerosis or a slipped disc.*

*According to his father, Walter Krug, he spent over US$50,000 on his son's treatment with no results. He decided to take him to the house which he heard of from a TV documentary. 'Alessandro now walks as if there was never anything wrong with him,' he said, 'He was cured by an* *invisible operation, herbs and spirit energy. I paid nothing except for the trips to Abadiania.'*

*His wife, Mrs Terezinha Krug, could not walk two steps from the unbearable pain caused by a malignant tumour in her womb. 'She was cured by a painless surgical elimination of the tumour without anaesthetic. An operation which took just five minutes.' Mr Krug explained.*

Personal Observation of the Author.

On the 12th of September 1996 I witnessed the removal of a large 7cm x 3 cm tumour from the right shoulder of a man of approximately 28 years of age. The man gave his name as Dr. Romeu Correia de Araujo Filho of Goiania, Goias. The operation was witnessed and observed by his colleague Dr. Divaldo Matos Sautana, a doctor of Gynaecology and Obstetrics from Goiania, and three other doctors.

The young doctor was asked to sit on a low stool. A house medium stood in front of him to provide current as Joao-in-entity made an incision approximately six centimetres long on the right deltoid (shoulder blade). Pieces of the growth were removed as he worked his way down to the main tumour until the it too was removed, almost in one piece. The cavity was then swabbed with "fluidated" water to sterilise the area. Two sutures closed the incision and the young doctor walked to the recovery room for post-operation rest.

The entire operation was closely observed by the four doctors and a multitude of people crowded into the main assembly hall. The tumour was given to the doctors for pathological testing.

In an interview with the doctors later, they were completely convinced of the authenticity of Joao and his entities and held no doubts that their colleague would make a full recovery.

From the House Testimonial Achives:

Gildo Felice lives in Mina Gerias and works for Banco Da Brazil.

"My illness began in Rio de Janeiro when I was working all day in air-conditioning. I had great difficulty in breathing and even with a transfer to Mina Gerias, my condition worsened. Finally I came to the point where I could hardly walk. I went to the doctors who conducted many tests but they could not diagnose anything.

I was sent to Sao Paulo to consult a specialist but he found nothing so I was hospitalised in University Hospital where I was tested and observed. Eventually I was sent home as incurable. I was now bedridden. I read about Joao in the newspaper and I instinctively knew he could cure me. I went to the house twice and the entity Jose Valdivino operated on me invisibly while I was standing in the crowd. I couldn't believe it but it was true.

*When I returned home I went to the doctors and asked for more tests the results of which showed no sign of the disease. This illness is now gone and my life with family and friends is just wonderful."*

Charles (name supplied but withheld by request) was a policeman for 28 years and then achieved a law degree. He developed a large tumour on his neck. He was operated on at Bela Horizonte hospital. It tested as malignant so he underwent chemotherapy and radiation treatment, twenty six sessions in all but the diagnosis was not good. The pain increased and the doctors reported that the cancer was spreading rapidly and recommended that he have more surgery.

His mother suggested a visit to see Joao and soon after, his wife had a dream about a hospital painted blue and white and received a message that this was the only place her husband could be cured. His father took him to the house and Joao greeted him, as he took hold of his hand he received an invisible operation. He was prescribed some herbs and he went home.

Charles ceased chemotherapy and within a week his hair was beginning to grow back. He returned to Abadiania to have a gallstone removed. The entity asked that when he return home he have an ultra sound test. The doctors were baffled; there was no inflammation and no gallstone but there was an internal mark where the stone was removed.

Charles at the time of writing was alive and well. The doctors had given him less than three months to live.

BRAZIL CENTRAL, 8 March 1995

***"Doctors Seek Help in House of Dom Inacio.***

*Not only simple folk seek the help of Joao Teixeira da Faria. People of all levels of society come to the house. Seron de Barros, a Neurologist living in Avenion Santa Caterina, 70. Vila Velha, underwent an invisible operation for renal calculus. 'Joao used no anaesthetic,' he said, 'and I could see nothing that could be considered charlatanism, on the contrary I saw a total devotion. I know the operation was completely successful.'*

*Doctor Nilton Ferreria, who works at the North Clinic Centre in Brazilia has been a Physiotherapist for 17 years. 'All my family have been treated or benefited in some way by the house. For the past five years I have been visiting the house and work as a volunteer in appreciation for the good works I and my family received.'*

TRIBUNA. Vitoria. 3 March '96.

***"Spiritual Treatment of Tumours.***

*Grazielle Zeltzer Gazzini, a happy and lively 18 year old girl entering her second year of college, suddenly had her life changed. She began feeling severe pain in the stomach and on one side of her head. She vomited every morning.*

*After many tests and examinations a final diagnosis was given: Grazielle had a brain tumour. If she underwent an operation she only had a twenty percent chance of survival and even if she did, she would only live another five months.*

*After undergoing radium and chemotherapy for three months, Grazielle did not walk or speak anymore and had to be fed through a probe. Her mother, Ida Maria Gazzini, decided to take her to Brasilia for further tests but the results were that there was no hope. 'Grazielle will never be normal again', the doctors said. In desperation, her mother took her to Abadiania, Goias, seeking the help of Joao de Deus.*

*Today, almost a year later, the young girl still doesn't go to school yet and needs a wheelchair to be moved, but she speaks, eats by herself and even quarrels with her brothers. She loves to dress up and wear lipstick. She is not totally cured yet but her mother is continuing the treatment and is sure she will make a full recovery."*

From the case files of Casa De Dom Inacio.

A woman (name given but withheld by request) who suffered traumatically from intense back pain. Doctors recommended she have three vertebrae removed and replaced with platinum. The problem was exacerbated by a swollen heart which caused her to faint frequently. She wore body bandages for eleven months and was barely able to move. *"My husband did not believe in Joao and his entities so one night I packed a bag and sneaked out to catch a bus to Abadiania,"* she revealed today.

*"Joao operated on my back and I became well. When I returned home my son took gravely ill so I went back to Abadiania to seek a cure for him. I cried when the Entity approached me. I did not ask for relief for myself, being grateful to receive a cure for my son. The Entity told me not to cry and asked if I would like to be healed as well. He removed my five dioptre glasses and threw them away. I was almost blind but he returned my sight and operated on my*

*heart. He said 'Whosoever brings their problems here and has faith will not have to take them back home," she said.*

*"I am only sad that I had to do it without my husband's support. But he is happy now that I am well and my son is better".*

Letter of Gratitude. Florence, 12 May 1996

*Dear Joao,*

*I am writing to thank you for the invisible operations I received last week at Abadiania. The entity, Dr. Augusto de Almeida, removed a large growth from my small intestine, growths from my right kidney and a small marble size growth from my throat. The intestinal growth was diagnosed in Australia some time ago but I was too afraid of medical surgery to have it removed. I can never thank you and your entities enough for making me better.*

*You may be interested to know that of the photos of my ill friends I took with me, all experienced phenomenal reactions on the day you reviewed them. Some had arthritic conditions which swelled alarmingly with redness and a great deal of fluid in the afflicted areas. Within a week, the swelling subsided and the conditions have all but disappeared. One, who has had chronic psoriasis of the skin for most of her adult life, experienced a marked reduction in the anger of the rash, and one who suffered a stroke seems to be recovering well.*

*Our visit to your healing hospital was a remarkable experience and we all thank you for dedicating your life to the relief of the suffering of your fellow man.*

*Yours sincerely*
*Caterina Pellegrino.*
*Via Del Corso, 16. Florence.*

Personal Interview, 26 July 1996.

"My name is Danilo Tibirica Nunes. I live at Joao Pessoa 1065/210 Porto Alegre, Brazil.

I was living in England, between 1990-92, when I became ill with cancer of the left breast. My operation included removal of a large tumour in the breast and the removal of numerous nodules from my lymphs under the arms. This was followed by chemotherapy and radiation. I was extremely sick during these treatments. The doctors warned me that I was only buying time because the cancer was malignant.

I went home to Brazil and eventually returned to work. Eight years later I became very ill again and my worst fears were realised when I was told I had a large cancer in the liver and throughout the bones of my chest and leg. There was little hope but I started chemotherapy again anyway as I did not want to die. A friend told me about Joao and I took the 35 hour bus journey to Abadiainia.

I have been operated on invisibly and the tumour in my liver is gone. The treatment of my bones is continuing with herbs and I am feeling so much better. If only I had known of this place before my first operation I would have been cured then without all that terrible therapy. Please use my name and address as a reference."

Signed Testimony, 26 October 1996

"I had been fighting cancer for eight years. I had one mastectomy (removal of the right breast) and for the past eight years I have been under the care of one of the most reputed cancer clinics in Europe - the Steiner Clinic in Bern, Switzerland.

With careful diet, drugs and injections I was able to slow down the spread of the disease but ultimately, by early 1995, the best I could expect was another twelve months of life. One day in April 1996, I was working in my herbalist shop when a woman called Caterina and her husband came in to ask if I would refer clients to her for Prana Therapy.

154

I sent her a client who reported back with glowing praise so I went for a consultation myself. Without telling her of my problems she diagnosed them all correctly. She told me I had two tumours on my neck, a larger one in my abdomen and small nodules on my left breast. She said she could help me but with so little time my only chance for a cure was a man she knew in Brazil.

In the first week in July 1996 I flew to Brazil with Caterina and her husband Robert and my best friend Mara who had a similar condition to mine. We were operated invisibly by Joao Teixeira da Faria, given herbs and returned to Italy. Caterina told us it would take a few months for a full recovery. During this time we both felt strange - periods of tiredness and high temperatures, modest pains and headaches but these effects were apparently normal and a part of the process.

On 11 October 1996 Mara and I went for our regular check-up at the Steiner Clinic. The doctors were amazed. Mara was declared totally clear of tumours and all of my tumours had disappeared except for one on my neck which was shrinking rapidly. The doctors said they had never seen anything like it in all their years at the clinic. Not only were the tumours gone but the disease seemed to be in remission. I am now living a healthy life without the fear of this terminal illness. " *Signed; Deanna Rovacchi. Florence, Italy.*

Signed Statement. 2 April 2000:

I was diagnosed with lymphoma four years ago. Eighteen months later I was diagnosed with adeno carcinoma. I was told I only had a few months to live. Since then I've worked hard on my health physically, emotionally and spiritually.

The first few weeks after arriving at the casa, I had a variety of experiences. At first I was restless, agitated, angry - I seemed to experience every emotion possible. The last three weeks here have been amazing; a calmness I haven't felt in a long time came upon me. Meditating in the current room has been wonderful.

The first unusual thing to happen to me occurred in the second current room. During my meditation I had intense pain in my back at the lower left ribs. I had scaring from a plurodices and the muscles there wouldn't stretch. The pain lasted perhaps five minutes then moved to the centre of my chest before vanishing. When I went outside I had a friend check my back and there was a red line about three inches long with a small round circle in the centre of it exactly where I had felt the pain.

The next amazing thing happened the following day. I was sitting in the current room in deep meditation when I was suddenly lifted a foot off the ground and thrown forward a few feet as if hit by lightning. I was stunned as I tried to scramble to my feet

For years now I have had extremely loose stool but since arriving in Abadiania it has returned to its normal healthy firm state. I also arrived with an immobile right thumb that had been swollen and red for two years - the symptoms of osteo arthritis. I'm delighted to report that I now have full movement of the thumb and it is pain free. *George Leppard - Sydney. Australia*

From the Author's Files.

We had been accompanying groups to Abadiania from Europe, USA and Australia for two years. One evening in February 1998 we had a call from the wife of a man who was in a Sydney hospital with cancer of the spine. We went to the hospital to visit but we were reluctant to encourage him to go to Brazil because of his intense pain, the discomfort he might suffer on the long trip and his attitude.

After reading the book he insisted on going. We were concerned so we sought the Entity's help by sending a photo of him in the hope that the would improve enough to endure the trip. Two weeks later he was much improved albeit with large daily doses of morphine to control the pain. He was changing too, there was a softness in his demeanour and a ray of hope in his eyes.

He refused chemotherapy that, the doctors said, would extend his life by six to twelve months. Within three weeks he was walking with the aid of crutches. By the time the trip was due to depart he was walking unaided.

He stayed three weeks in Abadiania, received two operations and spent a good deal of time in current. Two months later he reported for his medical check-up. The X-rays showed that the fast moving cancer had stopped. The cartilage that had been affected was still unchanged but the cancer had stopped growing.

That was over two years ago. He is off all pain-killers, works five days and tills his farm on the weekends but the real miracle is his changed attitude to life, God, his friends and his family.

The administration office at Abadiania has thousands of testimonies on file of successful cures. The video operators have recorded over 1500 hours of physical surgery. The vast library of tapes is available to anyone for purchase or examination.

It is difficult to calculate exactly how many people Joao and his entities have cured in total because the early life of Joao was not recorded and because of the incalculable numbers of absent healings they have done. Each person who comes to the centre for personal healing also brings with them two or three, sometimes multiple, photographs of friends and loved ones who request treatment by absent healing. Even a modest calculation would put the total in excess of fifteen million people treated!! The term *"Miracle Man"* is indeed a fitting title for Joao de Deus.

# Postscript

Joao and his entities can produce amazing results in healing sick minds and bodies but many illnesses are originally caused by incorrect living, both physically and spiritually. It is of little use to be healed if you do not change your living habits or the environment that bought about the ailment in the first place. It is up to each individual to help themselves prevent a reoccurrence with a serious look at their attitudes, environment and diet. There is no point in curing sclerosis of the liver if one continues to consume excessive alcohol!

*Avoid over-processed and fast foods.* The human body is a living organism and needs regular nourishment with live foods, not over-cooked, over-processed or 'fast foods'. Processed and fast foods contain chemicals, colourings, preservatives and enhancements with which the body was never meant to cope.

*Reduce the intake of cakes, white bread, biscuits* and other products made with white flour. There is no nourishment in them and they slow down the elimination system.

*Excessive coffee* over stimulates the nervous system and prevents absorption of food nutrients.

*Soft drinks and ice creams* contain sugar which poisons the bloodstream and shocks the body into temporary and unnatural energy highs.

*Alcohol destroys brain cells* that are never replaced.

*Smoking WILL cause lung cancer*, it might take a few years but smoking WILL KILL eventually.

*Artificial sweeteners.* Do not consume diet beverages or foods containing artificial sweeteners such as Aspartame or Nutri-sweet. There is irrefutable scientific evidence that these products can cause devastating illnesses now collectively called Aspartame Diseases.

*Unhindered natural light*. Get as much natural light each day as you can without over exposure but do not wear sunglasses or prescription lenes. Our bodies evolved as humans beings in natural light over millions of years. Our eyes take in light and colour to regulate, through the direction of the hypothalamus, our bodily functions. To artificially block out this vital energy source is inhibiting our body's natural ability to regulate and heal itself. Even car and window glass will block out essential UV light.

*Keep a simple diet with plenty of live foods*, salads, vegetables and a wide variety of fresh fruits. Don't eat too much red meat; alternate with chicken and fish.

*Reduce stress* by taking time out for yourself. Meditate in quiet surroundings as often as possible - communicate with your Creator. Live a life of peace and harmony with your fellow man and help others less fortunate than yourself whenever possible.

If God and the entities provide through Joao a second chance at this life it is important that you change your lifestyle to prevent your illness from returning.

Life is precious.

Take good care of yourself so you can enjoy it.

*Robert Pellegrino-Estrich.*

# Bibliography

Altea, Rosemary, *The Eagle and the Rose,* Bantam Books, New York 1995.

Alves, Carlos Joel Castro, *Uma Missao de Amor,* Editora Vitoria Ltda, Uberabe, Brazil1995.

Brennan, Barbara Ann, *Hands of Light,* Bantam Books, New York 1995.

Cayce, Edgar Evans, *Edgar Cayce on Atlantis,* Time Warner Books, New York 1968.

Carter, Mary Ellen and McGarey, William A., *Edgar Cayce On Healing,* Aquarian Press, New York 1972.

Carter, Mary Ellen, Under the Editorship of Hugh Lynn Cayce, *Edgar Cayce Modern Prophet,* A.R.E. Press,Virginia Beach 1967.

Carter, Mary Ellen and McGarey, William A., Edgar Cayce On Healing, Aquarian Press, New York 1991.

Edwards, Harry, *A Guide to the Understanding of Spiritual Healing,* Healer Publishing Company, Guildford, Surrey, 1974

Fuller, John G, *Arigo: Surgeon of the Rusty Knife,* Pocket Books, New York 1974.

Kardec, Allen, *The Book on Mediums or, Guide for Mediums and Invocators,* Samuel Weiser, York Beach 1970.

Jung, C.G. *Memories, Dreams, Reflections,* Fontana Press, London 1961.

Peck, M Scott, *The Road Less Travelled,* Arrow Books, New York 1986.

Povoa, Jose Liberato Costa, *Joao de Deus, Fenomeno de Abadiania,* Editora Vitoria Ltda., Uberaba, Brazil 1996.

Redfield, James and Adrienne, Carol, *The Celestine Prophecy an Experiential Guide,* Warner Books, New York 1995.

Reilly, Harold J. and Brod, Ruth Hagy, *The Edgar Cayce Handbook for Health Through Drugless Therapy,* 1975. A.R.E. Press, Virginia Beach 1975.

Roberts, Jane, *The Nature of Personal Reality*, Amber-Allen, San Raffael 1974.

Murphy, Michael,*The Future of the Body*, Jeremy P. Tarcher, Los Angeles 1992.

# ABOUT THE AUTHOR.

Robert Pellegrino-Estrich was led to the House of Dom Inacio by a dream in 1995. After a twenty-five year career in commerce, the logic of following the trail of a dream seemed unrealistic. He defied his logic and travelled to the high plateau region of central Brazil. What he saw there was to change his life forever. Within a few months he and his wife Caterina began accompanying terminally ill people across the Atlantic from Europe. His in-depth knowledge of Joao Teixeira da Faria, 'The Miracle Man', comes from the opportunity these many trips gave for him to study the man and his methods at the Casa de Dom Inacio as the book evolved.

Of the hundreds of 'hopeless cases' they accompanied to the sanctuary for treatment, most still live healthy active lives. Three months after their treatment most of them were cleared by their doctors, some of whom are the highest specialists in their fields of cancer, leukaemia, ophthalmology, osteopathy etc.

This demanding undertaking provided the opportunity to observe Joao-in-entity at first hand. His volunteer work in the centre enabled him to follow up the results of each client. Collectively they provided the basis of this book.

Despite countless scientific and medical studies and thousands of hours of video recordings, this is the first book written about Joao in a foreign language – initially in English and later in Italian, French and Portuguese. It is the only book that endeavours to explain the theories behind the amazing 'miracles'. Robert points to Joao Teixeira as the living proof of reincarnation, the survival of death, multi-dimensional existence and Man's ability to tap resources of healing long forgotten in this scientific age.

The author's contact address is:

P.O. Box 965, Double Bay N.S.W. 2028, Australia

Email: llight@ozemail.com.au

Website: www.johnofgod.com

## GARDEN OF GODS
By Peter O. Erbe

PETER O. ERBE

From the author of the highly acclaimed spiritual classic 'GOD I AM', comes 'GARDEN OF GODS', a deeply inspired collection of wisdoms, presented in the form of an 'open at any page' book, which may serve as a daily companion, offering profound insights.

GARDEN
OF GODS

ISBN: 0 9586707 0 6
Size 11.5 x 17.5 cm, 164 pages, PB.

**Excerpt:**

At your evening tide in the twilight of dusk
when the land is still, then go to the grove.
Let meadow and forest enfold you in their peace,
and when a calm balms your soul,
speak to ME in your heart and you shall find ME there.
And when we meet, the night bird shall hush -
your lips shall quiver in speechless wonder
and your heart tremble - in awe your knee shall bend,
for nothing so lovely have your eyes ever beheld
and no such love has your heart ever felt,
for you will find YOU - that which I AM.
And together as ONE, in silent wonderment,
shall we merge in the sweet ecstasy
of our communion.

# St. Germain
# TWIN SOULS
# &
# SOULMATES

Channelled by Azena
and Claire Heartsong

ISBN: 0 646 21150 1
A5, 160 pages, PB.

**This is a fascinating account of St. Germain's merging and ascension with his own soulmate Portia, and also an eye opener to the deeper spiritual mystery of this most misunderstood subject.**

"'Experiencing Christ-consciousness within yourself, loving unconditionally that which you are as you exist and abide in your reality at this point in time, creates the resonance within your being that attracts the identical essence within the opposite body of soul energy - your soulmate will manifest in physicality as a natural progression and merges with your energy and you with it. And as you merge together closer and closer and drink more and more of one another's cups, you become One, and you become one another's strength and one another's love. As this occurs, you experience what is called enlightenment. The physical expression of your soulmate automatically appears.
Your twin flame is the identical vibration of the vibration you emit in your personality Self in this your now moment. And if you will recognize that you already embody the principle of love, then you will merge with your soulmate and the merging of soulmates creates miracles."

# St. Germain
# EARTH'S BIRTH CHANGES

St. Germain
through Azena

Apart from revealing unknown, revolutionary facts about Earth's and humanity's history, St. Germain affords the reader elating and in depth insights into matters spiritual.

ISBN: 0 646 21388 1
A5, 280 pages, PB.

The upheavals, the unrest and torment within humanity at this time are the contractions and labour pains heralding a birth of an incomprehensible, cosmic magnitude. The decade before and after the turn of the century represent the culmination - the Harmonic Convergence - of a 200 million year evolutionary cycle: Earth and her children, in unison with the Solar system and thousands of galaxies, are birthing into a new dimension.

From the shores of eternal being, from the Council of Light, comes one called St. Germain to assist in this birthing process. As he bares his heart in love and compassion, rekindling an ancient memory, he transforms the prophecies of Old, of looming calamities and trepidation, into shining, new horizons without circumference. His words are carried by an air of urgency for the changes are imminent; quote: 'the acceleration is becoming exponential'. His gift to us is not approximate statement but the promise of fact: freedom for humanity. What is more, he unfolds a vision for humanity of such grandeur, that it renders the uninitiated speechless. If the historian and the scientist only as much as consider the information presented here, they will have to revise their certainties, for their facts are at risk. Unravelling a tapestry of dazzling beauty for humanity, the thrilling joy of St. Germain's message is contagious, is of effervescence and jubilance: the transition from separation to the union of Oneness with all Life - the age of Love -

*THE GOLDEN AGE OF GOD*

# MOTHER MARY'S TEACHINGS FOR THE NEW WORLD

Channelled by
Ileah Van Hubbard

ISBN: 0958670749
130 pages, PB

"Dearest Children of my heart,
I am come these days to awaken the hearts of humanity unto their Destiny, their journey back home into the heart and mind of God, from whence they have come in the beginning. The Journey has been long and arduous, as the Father has allowed you to experience life on your own, in separation, as was your desire. Now you have experienced all of life and, one by one, you are turning back to the Source.
This is a time of awakening – the reawakening of Mankind to his true existence as God/Man. This enlivened Spirit is the living Christ – the spark of life that has lain dormant for so long, for thousands of eons of time, the journey home."
Ileah Van Hubbard, who has given her life over to Mother Mary's guidance and direction, leads large events world-wide to anchor Her light and love into the people. To have Her teachings recorded, Mother Mary requested this book to be published.

Maree Moore

# The Masters of the Mystical Rose
### A History of the Grail Family

ISBN: 0958670757
731 pages, PB

## Inspirational – Educational – Historical

'The Masters of the Mystical Rose' presents a fascinating and in-depth account of the Grail family from Noah to Saint Germain – from the Knights Templar to the Royal House of Scotland. Meticulously re-searched, this book gathers the scattered pieces of the puzzle of history to form a meaningful picture, revealing stunning information and insights as to the Teachings of the Mystical Rose and the Masters who shaped the destiny of Mankind.

Did Atlantis and Lemuria really exist? Who was the mysterious Joseph of Arimathea? Did Merlin and Arthur exist? Where was Avalon? What was the Grail? Who were the Fisher Kings? Who was the Teacher of Righteousness of whom the Essenes wrote in the Dead Sea Scrolls? Learn the answers to these and hundreds of more questions.

This inspirational work ranks among the classics of human history.

# JOURNEY INTO THE NEW MILLENNIUM

### BY CLAIRVOYANT
### WENDY MUNRO

### A COSMIC ACCOUNT OF THE MILLENNIAL TRANSITION FOR HUMANITY AND PLANET EARTH

ISBN: 0 646 23473 0
A5, 230 pages, PB

## *A Compelling Prophecy*

As it has never been revealed before, this Sirian message explains the breathtaking process of the total physical and spiritual metamorphosis planet Earth and humanity are undergoing. In this light the prophecies take on a new meaning of hope and upliftment. The period between 1996 and 2012 will literally see the emergence of a new planet and a new species of mankind. This material will leave the reader with an in-depth understanding, the knowledge of the biological and spiritual implications of the millennial transition.

"Your new spirituality will remind you of the time when the desire to have joy, to experience and to create, to find the richness of Self reflected in the other, was the impulse that caused the original explosion from the Source of love; that original purpose for which you entered into this universe. In your new world you will experience heights of joy, expressed through the desire to create, unimaginable to your present mind. The congruency of your personal choices will create the new Garden of Eden where all live in harmony. This time, not a garden that was created for you, but by you. This is indeed the Promised Land. Your world will simply be, eternally, the external expression of your new radiant Self complete with a richness and vibrancy of colour.

With fear no longer part of your nature, your resonant vibration will lift you into multidimensional levels of awareness. You will not see the human form, but the radiant beauty of the soul's true essence. All living forms will be seen in their true garments. Your rivers will glisten; your birds will reveal colour beyond physical perception, and at last your trees and flowers will communicate with you. There will be no separation between any life form. The statement 'All is One' will be felt by the heart and soul".

# GOD I AM

## From Tragic To Magic

**For The Contemplative
And Discerning Reader**

ISBN: 0 646 05255 1
A5, 250 pages, PB

**This highly inspirational and undisputed classic speaks the language of the soul. 'GOD I AM' is a MUST for every sincere seeker of spiritual truth.**

There is a silent aching in the human soul for hope and joy, a void that longs to be filled. Hope is expectancy for something to come. To go beyond hope, to arrive at what we hope for - to lift the soul from the dense clouds of turmoil, sorrow and stagnation to the heights of clarity into light and Love - is our purpose here. This message tears the veil of make-believe and reveals our time, against all appearances, as the most exciting to be in. It inspires the soul to soar again – to release itself into freedom, the ongoing adventure of Spirit where all things are made new.

It is the purpose of this material to develop the magnificent tool of True Perception with which we align for the birth into the dawn of a new day in creation, the Age of Love. As the chrysalis is the bridge between caterpillar and butterfly, so is True Perception the bridge between separation and Oneness.

The universe with all its beings, in seen and unseen dimensions, join with us in the grandest of all celebrations, the jubilance of rebirth into Light - the dance of the Gods - for where Earth and we, as her children, go is the fulfilment of the soul's ancient cry:

We are coming Home

**Here is a brief sampling of reader's responses to 'GOD I AM'.**

**J.A. Janson, Alb., Canada:** I opened 'God I Am' and began to read. Within a few pages, I felt an urge to cry. The crying changed to raucous laughter and then abruptly back to crying again...I read the whole book through in one sitting, then I turned it right over and began again.

**G.M. Kunkle, OR, USA:**..read everything on metaphysics and wasn't ready for another book, but your explanations of things I've heard and read about for decades struck such cords and inspired me to go for broke like nothing else has.

**D. Ashby, N.Z.:**..read and reread 'God I Am'. It was a wonderful experience. From cover to cover I found it absolutely riveting.

**T. Sjoquist, N.Z.:** I recently read 'God I Am' and was so thoroughly enthralled as to have passed it on to several people...

**A. Evason, Minister, Vic., Australia:** I've been delighting in 'God I Am', borrowing it from my ex-wife when she isn't soaking it up.

**D.A. Hansen, WA, USA:** This is my first fan letter during my 69 years in the flesh. Your book 'God I Am' is SUPERB.

**M. Grosshuesch, CO, USA:** I just finished reading 'God I Am' and want to express my appreciation to you...There is so much for me to think and learn about that I look forward to my second reading. You are a profound influence on my life - I am in your debt.

**L. Meybohm, W.A., Australia:** Thank you for writing 'God I Am'. You have helped me to turn the most important corner in my life and for this I am truly grateful. God bless you forever more.

**M. Hampson, Vic., Australia:** I write in gratitude...Having just read 'God I Am' I felt inspired and inwardly strengthened at the poetic beauty and accuracy with which you describe (my) our life purpose and soul intent.

**K. Smiles, N.S.W., Australia:** I would like to express my deep gratitude for this wonderful book...and thank you for the eloquence, strength and undeniable genius you have displayed in the writing of this book, which is, in itself, a work of art.

**J. Murray, Life Directions Counseling Cr., WA, USA:** My congratulations. I believe you have written the NEWest Testament. This book is the Owner's Manual for our times. I have read the epilog over at least five times. It is the most complete work I have ever seen - and the highest level, metaphysically and spiritually.

**K. Erickson, AZ, USA:** My husband and I wish to thank you for 'God I Am'. It truly works magic. For me it was something I have never felt from a book before. As I started to read it in solitude I felt a thrill emanating from deep within, exploding into a joy that I can only describe as my soul responding in recognition of the Truths. My husband was amused at my reaction, until it happened to him.

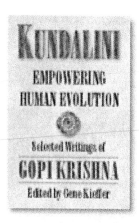

# KUNDALINI

## EMPOWERING HUMANEVOLUTION

Selected Writings of
### GOPI KRISHNA
Edited by Gene Kieffer

ISBN: 0958670722, 300 pages, PB

"In all my writings, I have sown the seeds of what I consider to be the most pressing need of mankind - namely, information about the evolutionary mechanism in human beings, slowly drawing the race to a golden future of harmony, peace and happiness."

Gopi Krishna

A world-renowned yogi, Gopi Krishna reveals the remarkable source of psychic energy that lies within us all. Known only to the ancients by such names as the "sixth sense" and the "philosopher's stone", this extraordinary life-force can be tapped to provide an inexhaustible reserve of energy and knowledge.

Drawn from the celebrated writings of Gobi Krishna, the founder of the Kundalini, Empowering Human Evolution, is the definitive guide to understanding the mystery of Kundalini and awakening this source of inner light, expanded consciousness and increased creativity in our lives. In these powerful essays, Krishna shows how we can use Kundalini to guide our private and public lives, as well as to answer the most urgent questions of our troubled age.

Gene Kieffer is director and president of the Kundalini Research Foundation, which he helped establish at the request of Gopi Krishna. He is longtime member of the Academy of Religion and Psychical Research, and serves on the advisory board of the Encyclopidia of Evolution.